To young people everywhere who, when con
an urgent social need in their community
around the world, decide to take actio
choose to make a difference.

■ ■ ■

This great little book is about young people who have proved that it is possible to change things for the better, to make a difference. It really belongs to them, just as the world does. We are very proud to know them and to know that there are many more like them.

Sir David Bell
Chairman Pearson Inc & Financial Times Group
Chairman International Youth Foundation

OUR TIME IS NOW
YOUNG PEOPLE CHANGING THE WORLD

ACKNOWLEDGMENTS

This book would not have been possible without the combined efforts of a dedicated group of individuals spanning five continents and numerous time zones.

Special thanks go to Mark Nieker of the Pearson Foundation, who upon hearing of the concept for the book, immediately understood its importance and agreed to publish it. Our gratitude additionally extends to the rest of the Pearson team – to Erik Gregory for his creativity and superlative design talents, to Trish Medalen for her tireless editing and attention to detail, to Wendy Darling for overseeing the production process, and to Steve Brown for his videography skills.

This project would also never have been realized without the generous support of the Nokia Corporation. Our heartfelt thanks go to Martin Sandelin, Kimmo Lipponen, Veronica Scheubel, and the other members of the Nokia Community Involvement team.

A debt of gratitude is owed the book's two writers, Christy Macy and Sheila Kinkade, who persevered in capturing the details of each story, and to IYF staff Alan Williams and Ashok Regmi, who contributed their creativity and insights to many aspects of the book's creation.

To each of our guest essayists, and to all of those who are quoted herein, we are extremely grateful for your time and insights into the powerful role of today's youth. We would also like to acknowledge the invaluable contributions of the many organizations that nominated potential candidates for the book.

To Archbishop Desmond Tutu, we cannot thank you enough for introducing and framing these stories in relation to the larger role we all can play in making the world a better place. Similarly, we honor Jim Toole, Ph.D., whose afterword provides a heartwarming and insightful analysis of the lessons these stories have to offer.

And last, but not least, our admiration and sincere thanks go to all of those young people who agreed to share their stories with us and with the world. You humble and inspire us with your passion and dedication to improving the lives of others.

William S. Reese
President & CEO
International Youth Foundation

OUR TIME IS NOW

NOMINATING ORGANIZATIONS

We are grateful to the following national and international organizations for nominating young leaders for consideration in this book:

African Youth Alliance Project – Uganda

Balkan Children and Youth Foundation

Consuelo Foundation (Philippines)

Family Health International (USA)

Foundation for Young Australians

Free The Children (Canada)

Horizons/Population Council

ImagineNations Group

Inter-American Development Bank

Kids&Future (Republic of Korea)

LEAP Africa (Nigeria)

Mobility International USA

National Children's Bureau (United Kingdom)

National Council for Child and Youth Development (Thailand)

New Perspectives Foundation (Russia)

The Prince's Trust (United Kingdom)

Search for Common Ground

Source of the Nile Award Uganda

Uganda Girl Guides

Uganda Red Cross Society

Uganda Scout Association

United Nations Environment Programme

W.K. Kellogg Foundation (United States)

The World Bank

Youthreach (India)

TABLE OF CONTENTS

Foreword: Archbishop Desmond Tutu

SECTION ONE
Passion for a Cause: What Sparks It?

SECTION TWO
Different Roads to the Same Destination: A Better World

OUR TIME IS NOW

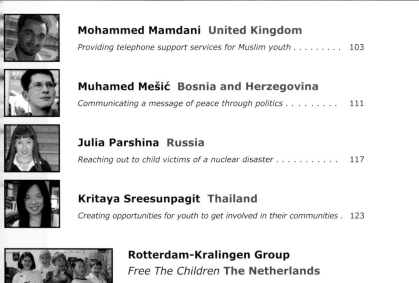
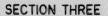
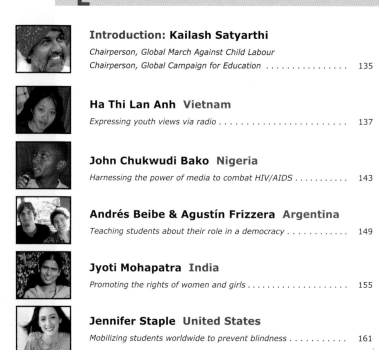

OUR TIME IS NOW

If you are neutral in situations of injustice, you have chosen the side of the oppressor. If an elephant has its foot on the tail of a mouse and you say that you are neutral, the mouse will not appreciate your neutrality.

– Archbishop Desmond Tutu

ARCHBISHOP DESMOND TUTU

NOBEL PEACE PRIZE LAUREATE
FOUNDER THE DESMOND TUTU PEACE CENTRE

Foreword
Why This Book? Why Now?

Most of us can remember an experience or person that helped shape our view of the world and our place in it. When I was a child, I had tuberculosis and spent nearly two years in a hospital. Once a week, a priest, a well-known anti-apartheid activist who happened to be white, would visit me. At the time, I was unaware of the impact his act of caring would have on my consciousness. This champion of the dispossessed touched my life deeply with his example of goodness.

Throughout this book, you will read similar stories of young people whose lives and worldview were fundamentally shaped by a person or event, and who today are reaching out to others, in much the same manner as that priest reached out to me.

Collected here are stories of passionate, committed young leaders who chose not to look the other way when they saw a problem – the shame experienced by a person with HIV/AIDS, the poisoning of a sacred river, the frustration of a nation's citizens in the face of a national crisis, the exclusion of the physically disabled. These are young people who choose to take a stand.

As a result of their efforts, low-income women are building small businesses, and students are learning about their role in a democracy. Once-illiterate adults are learning to read, and a host of other urgent needs are being met.

These young visionaries are representative of thousands of their peers in communities large and small around the globe. Youth are uniquely equipped to change the world because they dream. They choose not to accept what is, but to imagine what might be. Many of the youth you will read about here began their service work with little to no training, no money, and few connections to those who might help. Still, they persevered and successfully enrolled others in their efforts.

OUR TIME IS NOW

THE DESMOND TUTU
PEACE CENTRE

CAPE TOWN, SOUTH AFRICA

The Desmond Tutu Peace Centre's Leadership Academy seeks to nurture and develop visionary leadership among young people and women.
For further information, visit:
www.tutu.org

While this book focuses on the motivations and accomplishments of more than thirty young leaders, it's also about the hundreds of young people who work side by side with them. As you will discover, those profiled, while leaders in their own right, humbly describe themselves as sparks that ignite other people's passion for social justice.

Leading is about serving others. In today's fast-paced, competitive society, it may seem unrealistic to live your life in service of a greater good, but that's just what our world needs most. What are the attributes of a leader? Integrity. Compassion. Gentleness. Magnanimity. When Nelson Mandela emerged from twenty-seven years in prison, what the world saw was not anger and bitterness, but a readiness to forgive and pursue reconciliation. These are the qualities we all need to aspire to and those that a true leader models for us.

This book seeks to foster connections between today's youth leaders. Far too often, young leaders work in isolation, unaware of their peers carrying out similar activities around the world. It's also about sharing good ideas. Included here is information and advice on how to strengthen youth-led – or, indeed, any grassroots – projects. Readers will gain insights into how to advocate their cause, raise money, plan an event, mobilize other youth, network, and collaborate with others.

What are the lessons in these stories? First and foremost is the power of every individual to make a difference in his or her community. All you need is an idea and the will to make it happen. Second is the growing contribution of today's youth in making our world a better place. The growth of civil society around the world and new

technologies, including the Internet, are providing young people with greater opportunities to get engaged, network with one another, and have their voices heard. Young people are taking action like never before. This is good news for all of us.

And a final, critical lesson is the vital role that each of us can play in supporting youth-led efforts. In these pages, you will read of the nonprofit leaders, business people, government officials, and community members who rallied behind these young leaders and their causes. Some provided encouragement. Others offered their time, their expertise, their financial support, or other key services.

Goodness, I believe, is inherent in all human beings. While bad news abounds in today's world, I believe that compassion and gentleness are the norm. Who hasn't experienced the wonderful feeling of doing something good for another? In that moment, we recognize our common humanity and reflect the light that is in each of us.

I have a dream that one day we will all come to realize that we are part of the same family. While our world is one of great divides – racial and ethnic divides, economic and political divides – we share the same earth and breathe the same air. It could very well be that today's global challenges have the capacity to bring us closer together than ever before.

To each of you who reads this book: I encourage you to dream, to care, to be compassionate, and to let yourselves soar with your ability to create positive change in a world that desperately needs you. **Your time is now!** ∎

Passion for a Cause:
What Sparks It?

MARIAN WRIGHT EDELMAN

FOUNDER AND CHIEF EXECUTIVE OFFICER
CHILDREN'S DEFENSE FUND

This book is filled with profiles of extraordinary young people – you and your peers – who are making a difference around the world. Our global community is on the brink of many wonderful possibilities even as we face many challenges. We already know we have the resources and technology to make the world fit and safe for all young people. We just need the will. And all across the world we can see the growing movement of people determined to bring about change. This movement will be led by a new generation of servant-leaders just like you: people who look at the world, see wrongs that should be righted, and take action.

I grew up in Bennettsville, South Carolina, a small town in the segregated American South. My father was a Baptist preacher, and my mother – like so many women around the world – was a church and community leader and a true organizer. As a child I learned to serve others and try to change the world around me for the better by the example my parents set every day. Service was as essential a part of my upbringing as eating, sleeping, and going to school. Whenever my parents saw a need, they tried to respond.

Children's Defense Fund

For over thirty years, the Children's Defense Fund has worked to make sure that no child gets left behind in the United States.

Marian Wright Edelman with Congressional Representative George Miller and Senator Christopher Dodd, principal cosponsors of The Act to Leave No Child Behind, comprehensive legislation for U.S. children.

There were no Black homes for the aged in Bennettsville, so Daddy began one across the street, for which he and Mama and we children cooked and served and cleaned. Finding another child in my room or a pair of my shoes gone was far from unusual, and twelve foster children followed my sister and me and three brothers as we left home. We were told that the world had a lot of problems; that Black people had an extra lot of problems, but that we were able and obligated to struggle and change them; that being poor was no excuse for not achieving; and that extra intellectual and material gifts brought with them the privilege and responsibility of sharing with others less fortunate. In sum, we learned that service is the rent each of us pays for living. It is the very purpose of life and not something you do in your spare time.

The mission of the Children's Defense Fund is to Leave No Child Behind and to ensure every child a Healthy Start, a Head Start, a Fair Start, a Safe Start, and a Moral Start in life and successful passage to adulthood with the help of caring families and communities. Part of our mission is to empower all young people to embrace their responsibility to make a difference in themselves, their community, and the world. I know that young people who believe they can make a difference can change the world because I've seen it happen.

My generation was blessed beyond measure to experience and help bring transforming change to the South and to America in partnership with mentor-leaders like Dr. Martin Luther King, Jr. I first heard Dr. King speak in person during my senior year in college. He was just 31, but had already gained a national reputation during the successful Montgomery Bus Boycott. He became a mentor and friend. It's important to remember that Dr. King did not do it alone. Children desegregated public schools and stood up to police dogs and firehoses. Students sat-in at segregated restaurants and began voter registration drives. Young people marched and went to jail all across the South. The civil rights movement of the 1950s and 1960s was truly intergenerational.

Most people remember Dr. King as a great leader. I do too. I also remember him as someone able to admit how often he was afraid and unsure about his next step. But faith prevailed over fear, uncertainty, fatigue, and sometimes depression. It was his human vulnerability and ability to rise above it that I most remember. In this, he was not different from many Black Americans whose credo has been to make "a way out of no way."

You can hear the same credo all around the world. The language may be different, but the conviction is the same. It's a credo that applies to anyone who is committed to change. That is the key to taking part in any struggle for justice: learn to make a way out of no way. Believe you can make a difference and then do it. Take that first step in faith, and face up to your uncertainty and doubts with new determination and the knowledge that you are never alone in the struggle for justice. Never, *never* give up. Remember the saying that "there is not enough darkness in the world to snuff out the light of even one small candle." So let your light shine. ■

STELLA AMOJONG

Working to prevent teen pregnancy

KENYA

There is nothing as frustrating when, as a child, you desperately need some piece of information but are unable to get it. This is what happened to a friend of mine in school when she started experiencing her monthly periods. The best source of information should have been at home, but when my friend asked her mother what was happening to her body, she was thrashed and told to shut up! My poor buddy could not take the embarrassment for a week. She skipped school. And this is what happened every month until the teachers gave her the information she needed.

Almost the same thing happened to me when I was 13. My aunt would just stare at me as if I had gone out of my mind asking her about reproductive health issues. Her look told me, 'You are too young to know these things!' But fortunately, my mother provided me with all the information I needed about body changes, puberty, and sex. But that set me thinking: Why not share the information I had with my schoolmates?

– Stella Amojong

Stella counsels a teen mother.

In Kenya, more than a thousand teenage girls become pregnant every day. Most received little education at home or school concerning their reproductive health and issues involving sexuality. More than half undergo an illegal abortion. Many are expelled from school and never offered a chance to resume their education.

Such alarming statistics have long fueled the activist drive of Stella Amojong. From a makeshift office in her modest, three-room home in Eldoret, Kenya, Stella is slowly transforming the attitudes of local parents, school administrators, church leaders, and government officials toward reproductive health education.

Students prepare to "graduate" from an ATM-sponsored reproductive health education program.

As program coordinator of the Advocates for Teenage Mothers Group (ATM), an organization she founded in 2003, Stella has fought an uphill battle to promote the rights of young women to access essential knowledge concerning their reproductive health. Denied such knowledge, thousands of girls, some as young as 14, end up as single parents each year, most of them living in poverty, according to Stella. The HIV/AIDS crisis has magnified the situation because, Stella notes, now one poor decision can result in a death sentence.

Today, ATM is widely recognized in Eldoret, a fast-growing city of 400,000, for its efforts to promote the healthy development of teenage girls and young mothers. Over the past two years, the organization has distributed nearly 15,000 educational flyers and pamphlets; trained 125 youth as peer educators; provided reproductive health counseling to over 700 students; reached more than 2,200 middle school students with its reproductive health curriculum; trained more than 130 young mothers in micro-enterprise skills; and launched a new program aimed at combating the spread of HIV/AIDS.

The group's track record is also gaining visibility outside the country, with Stella having been nominated to receive an Ashoka Fellowship. Headquartered in the U.S., Ashoka identifies and invests in social entrepreneurs with unprecedented ideas for change in their communities. Says Ashoka East Africa representative Deborah Kaddu-Serwadda, "Stella's work is addressing a critical issue among youth today. The strategic combination of several approaches proves Stella's exceptional entrepreneurial quality and creativity."

Providing Essential Health Information

Stella's passion for helping young girls make healthy life choices is deeply rooted in her experiences as a teenager whose own family only reluctantly shared vital information about reproductive health.

In an atmosphere in which discussing sexuality with adults was often taboo, Stella soon discovered that most youth received information largely from their peers, magazines, popular films, and pornographic videos. Young people lacked not only knowledge, but also the skills to discuss sex-related topics with health care providers and to assert themselves with partners, she says.

Stella's commitment intensified when, at 17, she experienced the death of a close friend as a result of an illegal abortion. Recognizing the need for young women to take charge of their bodies – and their futures – Stella founded "GirlPower," a student-run organization providing young girls with reproductive health information and assistance in obtaining part-time jobs.

Stella's commitment intensified when, at 17, she experienced the death of a close friend as a result of an illegal abortion.

Early on in her work, Stella understood that reproductive health messages are often best communicated to young people by their peers. "Many girls were in a dilemma when it came to understanding their bodies," recalls Stella. "It turned out they were more receptive and comfortable talking among themselves about so-called 'sensitive' issues than waiting for parents and teachers to provide answers."

Developing a Comprehensive Approach

Through ATM, Stella seeks to engage youth themselves and the community as a whole in efforts to educate young people about important reproductive health issues and the risks of too-early and unprotected sexual activity. "Our strategies are multipronged, youth led, and interactive," explains Stella, who learned at a young age the importance of persistence and self-reliance. The oldest of five children, Stella cared for her siblings following the death of her parents. Now a wife and mother of three children, she devotes up to forty hours each week to managing ATM activities.

The sitting room of Stella's home serves as ATM's primary office space. Twice a week, ATM staff and volunteers meet here to plan upcoming activities and evaluate their progress. The makeshift office contains books, manuals, and other publications on women's rights and reproductive health, along with a TV and VCR for showing educational videos. A prized piece of equipment is a stereo that the group uses regularly to rehearse its dance- and drama-based "edutainment" programs. Stella's bedroom houses a computer, printer, and scanner, and serves as a storage area for ATM's educational outreach materials. Another room, the "rescue

Medical personnel provide basic health care to Eldoret residents during an ATM-organized visit to the area.

Youngsters communicate reproductive health messages during a community event sponsored by ATM.

Stella helps a teen mother to package bread. Proceeds from the ATM bakery project support the program and young mothers.

shelter," is set up with bunk beds where Stella often hosts pregnant girls who either have been forced to leave their homes or have run away. While Stella dreams of one day acquiring a formal office space, the current setup allows the group to function on a lean budget ranging from U.S.$1,500 to U.S.$3,000 a year.

Currently, ATM has nine staff and ten volunteers – all under the age of 22. Staff members describe Stella as the organization's "mother"; someone they look to for advice, direction, and encouragement. The majority of staff are trained peer educators who provide information and counseling to ATM clients, visit local schools to conduct group discussions, carry out advocacy campaigns, and meet with community leaders and policymakers to convey their message of youth empowerment. While ATM can't afford to pay most of its staff a regular salary, it does help out with staff members' transportation, housing, rent, and food costs.

Early on in ATM's work, Stella took care to establish a diverse and committed board of directors, comprised of medical practitioners, teachers, prominent elders in the community, religious leaders, and journalists. The board members meet regularly and provide assistance based on their respective fields. Given their stature within the community, board members act as bridge-builders, making the case for enhanced reproductive health education to groups that remain reluctant to embrace ATM's message.

Staff members describe Stella as the organization's "mother"; someone they look to for advice, direction, and encouragement.

ATM's services have evolved over time to address diverse, yet interconnected, needs. A core focus is reaching out to young women who have become pregnant or who are already mothers. Through the "Wind of HOPE: Education for All Teen Mothers" project, ATM offers young mothers academic tutoring, career counseling, and assistance in completing their secondary-school educations. As a result of ATM's advocacy efforts, in 2004–2005 school administrators allowed more than thirty young mothers – previously expelled from school as a result of their pregnancies – the chance to return.

ATM also works to increase livelihood opportunities for young mothers. Two years ago, the group set up a modest baking enterprise in Eldoret's main marketplace, where young mothers receive training in how to make cakes and *mandazi*, or fried bread, and sell them to people on their way to work. Stella herself often gets up at five in the morning to help the girls prepare. The bakery generates roughly three hundred Kenyan shillings a day (the equivalent of U.S.$4), which is used to provide small allowances for the girls and to support ATM activities.

Another project, "Your Life, Your Choice," targets students, ages 10 to 19, and teachers through providing schools with a reproductive health curriculum covering topics such as relationships, disease prevention, sexual abuse, and effective communication. ATM received help in developing the curriculum from the Centre for Development and Population Activities (CEDPA), an international organization based in the United States. Stella discovered CEDPA and many other valuable resources through surfing the Internet. Local organizations also help train young people to serve as peer educators, who lead discussions on health and sexuality, perform songs and skits, and engage participants in role-playing exercises. Materials are also made available on reproductive health issues, and information is provided to students on where to go for checkups.

Through its recently launched "Compassion" project, ATM seeks to prevent the spread of HIV/AIDS among youth.

Through its recently launched "Compassion" project, ATM seeks to prevent the spread of HIV/ AIDS among youth, while providing home-based support to people infected with the disease and their families. It also works to reduce the stigma experienced by those with HIV/AIDS through community sensitization campaigns.

Changing Attitudes

As her work with ATM has progressed, Stella has come to realize that its success depends largely on changing the attitudes of key constituents within the local community, including government representatives, school authorities, church officials, parents, and young people themselves. Slowly, over time, she and her peers have worked to educate and enlist the support of each of these groups.

ATM members advocate for greater access to antiretroviral drugs for HIV-positive persons.

Yet getting through to them remains a challenge. Stella admits that gaining access to government authorities and convincing them of the importance of offering reproductive health education in schools has been extremely difficult. Without broad-based government support, Stella's appeals to individual schools have met with limited success. "Some of the school heads are very conservative and give us a hard time. They are not in favor of providing this kind of information to their students, even though the teachers are eager to support us." Still,

ATM members use drama to deliver vital health information at a community meeting.

ATM has succeeded in convincing fifteen schools to introduce its reproductive health curriculum.

To make its messages more accessible, ATM incorporates entertainment into its educational outreach. Just as community elders have long used storytelling to impart knowledge, ATM has developed songs, dances, and short dramas that capture the realities and consequences of irresponsible sexual activity, including the risks of pregnancy and HIV/AIDS. Such an approach is not only culturally acceptable, but helps ATM reach out to illiterate audiences.

Given that local church leaders were opposed to teaching reproductive health in schools, Stella opted first to approach smaller Christian groups that were more receptive to ATM's work. In one community, Kamukunji, ATM's efforts to enlist the support of religious leaders is finally paying off, with the church there having invited ATM staff to offer seminars to its parishioners on parental responsibility, effective communication, and HIV/AIDS prevention. As a result of ATM's outreach, another church group has started visiting orphanages, taking food to young single mothers, and visiting teens in the hospital.

Stella attributes her success at convincing others to change their attitudes to sheer persistence

and her passion for preventing young girls from making poor life choices that could trap them and their children in a lifetime of poverty. Stella's warm smile, soft-spoken demeanor, and integrity make her easy to like – and trust. Yet beneath her warm exterior lies a woman of grit and conviction.

Overcoming Challenges

While proud of what she and the others have accomplished, Stella admits that many obstacles remain. The group's work is carried out largely through the efforts of young volunteers who lack formal training. "As an organization, our chances of attracting outside financial support are hampered by the training needs of our staff and volunteers," she says. "Our personnel need to be educated in areas like monitoring, evaluation, management, and reporting."

Stella attributes her success at convincing others to change their attitudes to sheer persistence...

Funding remains a constant challenge. ATM is financed largely through membership fees paid by community members, although their contributions vary from year to year, making it difficult for ATM to conduct any long-range planning. Each individual in ATM's current roster of three hundred members pays an annual fee of just over U.S.$2.60. Its fifty "golden members" pay U.S.$6.60 annually, and an additional U.S.$1.30 monthly fee.

Recognizing that increasing reproductive health awareness among young women is an urgent need around the world, in 2005 Stella teamed up with a young women's rights advocate in India, Jyoti Mohapatra (see profile, page 155), whom she met at a conference. Together, the two applied for a grant through the International Youth Foundation and were awarded U.S.$3,300 for their project. As a result, ATM has now expanded its services to include teaching proper hygiene to girls in school; while young women in India are benefiting from enhanced life skills education based largely on ATM's approach.

In the future, Stella hopes to establish a network of slum-based resource centers in Kenya and elsewhere in East Africa that will provide at-risk youth with reproductive health information and training. Says Stella, "I dream of an organization whose social message will have permeated all sectors of society in offering solutions to the many problems facing young people." ∎

Youth take part in a peer education training held by ATM.

Stella met Jyoti Mohapatra (right), a founder of the Meena Clubs in India, at a conference. The two are now collaborating on a project that enables each to adapt the methods of the other in better addressing the health needs of young women in their respective countries.

"Stella Amojong's interventions at different levels are helping unwed mothers get back into school and the mainstream of society. She is giving these young women new hope and a second chance in life. . . . The youth of East Africa need more individuals like Stella to hold their hands through the challenges of teenage-hood."

Deborah Kaddu-Serwadda
Regional Representative Ashoka East Africa
Kampala, Uganda

ADVICE FROM STELLA ON:

Effectively Managing a Social-Interest Project

- **Form an advisory group or board of directors to provide you with guidance and access to valuable resources.** ATM's board of directors is made up of teachers, parents, health professionals, and other important leaders in the community. The board meets twice monthly or when an important issue needs to be discussed.

- **Involve others in decision-making.** Stella is careful to engage staff, volunteers, and those young people being served in making important decisions. "Don't make decisions for young people," she cautions.

- **Engage members of the community in your efforts.** Invest the time and energy needed to convince key community members of the importance of your mission. Stella has worked hard over the years to educate government and religious leaders about the needs of young women in the community.

- **Know your audience and deliver your message in appropriate ways.** With many community members not knowing how to read or write, Stella and her peers developed songs and plays to convey their message concerning the risks of failing to educate teens about health issues, including pregnancy and sexually transmitted diseases such as HIV/AIDS.

- **Conduct research and network through the Internet.** Stella carefully researched international organizations that produce materials and offer funding in the area of reproductive health awareness training. Several such groups have provided her with free materials, and one even helped ATM create a curriculum that is now being used in schools.

- **Maintain the integrity of your principles and be persistent.** Stella credits much of her success to her deep personal commitment to improving opportunities for young women in Eldoret. Whether talking to a reluctant government official or an angry parent whose daughter has become pregnant, Stella maintains her composure and is respected for her drive and her professionalism.

SADIQA BASIRI

Providing girls with access to education

AFGHANISTAN

Schools are needed for girls in all provinces in Afghanistan to stop the exceedingly high rate of illiteracy and ignorance. We also need to raise awareness of women's universal rights and educate women so they know what Islamic law and international human rights laws allow for women. We must change people's minds and teach them that women are human beings who have equal rights in society. If discrimination is eliminated, there would be less violence against women, and they would be free to make decisions.

– Sadiqa Basiri

Schools for girls in Afghanistan were closed down during the Taliban's rule.

In 1986, during the violent Soviet occupation of Afghanistan, 6-year-old Sadiqa Basiri fled the country with her family. As Soviet soldiers searched their truck at a checkpoint, Sadiqa was terrified that she and her brother, sisters, and mother would be discovered, but eventually they made it over the border to Pakistan. So began a difficult decade of life as a refugee, cut off from friends and familiar surroundings. After months of sharing a rug on the floor with her siblings in an otherwise empty room in the refugee camp, Sadiqa moved with her family to the Pakistani city of Tahkal, where life became more comfortable. Sadiqa and her sisters attended school regularly, an opportunity she took for granted at the time. It would be years before she fully appreciated her good fortune.

Sadiqa's life took a new turn in 1994, when, in the ninth grade, she accompanied her family on a three-month visit back to her home village of Godah in eastern Afghanistan. At first, Sadiqa enjoyed herself in the familiar surroundings, hiking in the mountains and fishing in nearby streams. But soon she came to the realization that her years away from home, and the education she had received, made her noticeably different.

Students who had never learned to read or write attend class in a school that Sadiqa established.

She ran back to the house to talk with her father, who confirmed that none of the girls or women in the town had ever attended school.

One day, local villagers approached Sadiqa with a series of questions. They asked what her life had been like while she was away, what she thought of school, what the teachers looked like, and whether she was allowed to go to school alone. "They asked me questions I will never forget, and I got very sad," Sadiqa recalls. She ran back to the house to talk with her father, who confirmed that none of the girls or women in the town had ever attended school. That day Sadiqa sat alone, trying to imagine what life would be like if she weren't allowed to go to school.

Sadiqa's village reflected the harsh realities in Afghanistan at the time. The Taliban, an ultra-conservative religious sect that would rule most of Afghanistan during the mid- and late 1990s, was just beginning to implement its repressive policies. They would eventually ban women from the workplace and sharply restrict girls' education. The situation has improved considerably since the fall of the Taliban in 2001 and the establishment of a democratically elected government in Afghanistan. Yet, while five million youth now attend school, the country still has one of the world's lowest literacy rates. In some areas, up to 98 percent of Afghan girls and women can't read or write, and more than a million school-age girls are unable to attend school.

The barriers to girls' education are many and deeply rooted. Decades of civil war have decimated the country's infrastructure and contributed to widespread poverty. The Taliban regime closed most girls' schools, and a lack of books, transportation, and trained teachers continues to pose formidable challenges. Yet perhaps the greatest barrier is that girls are not as valued in society as their male counterparts, due to age-old cultural attitudes and traditions.

"A boy baby's birth is celebrated at least three times, but for a girl baby, the parents and the rest of the family are not even happy to give her a name," Sadiqa explains. "Parents do not invest in girls' education since they consider their daughters part of another family – [that of] the man whom she will marry."

Due to lack of funding, some girls' schools are housed in tents. These students are attending Sadiqa's Noorkhal school in Wardak province.

Turning a Dream to Build Schools into Reality

Eight years after her first visit home to Afghanistan, Sadiqa returned to Godah in 2002 with the goal of improving educational opportunities for women and girls. Tapping the skills and experience she gained during previous work with the Afghan Women's Educational Center and later at the Afghan Women's Network, Sadiqa and two friends founded the Omid Learning Center. The Center's mission was to create a model school that could then be duplicated across the entire country. Translated from the Persian language, *omid* means "hope," which is exactly what Sadiqa and her colleagues were determined to provide to their new students.

But getting started was not easy. Working on a tight budget, Sadiqa planned to run the school out of her family's home. She had saved enough money from her previous jobs to pay the salaries for two teachers and one principal, as well as purchase textbooks, pens and pencils, and school bags for the students.

Finding qualified female teachers proved to be a bigger challenge. After a long and frustrating search in eighteen surrounding villages, Sadiqa was forced to hire two male teachers. Her last and greatest obstacle was persuading the community that a girls' school was even necessary.

Some of the students who are benefiting from Sadiqa's Omid Learning Center gather in their classroom. Omid means "hope" in Persian.

To raise awareness in the community about the need to educate girls, Sadiqa invited all of the women and mullahs, or religious leaders, in the surrounding area to a special event at her home. There she told them stories of refugees in Pakistan and the United States who had become lost, were unable to secure housing or food for their families, or were trapped in their own homes – all because they couldn't read. She also talked about how the Qur'an, the sacred Islamic text around which the Muslim community's religious and social life revolves, valued learning – for everyone.

"I quoted the Qur'an about the need for education, and how it is not a matter of choice, but an order from Mohammed," Sadiqa says. "People were shocked," she recalls. "When I shared these things, women, including grandmothers, started to cry and came up to me to kiss my hands. They told me, 'We are too old, we are 80, but our daughters are not too old.'" Sadiqa told them that it was not time to cry but to act, and informed the crowd that registration for the girls' school would begin at 8 A.M. the following day.

Afghanistan has one of the lowest literacy rates in the world, and the need to build more schools and hire more teachers is urgent.

Her fears that no one would show up were soon put to rest, as a long line of girls arrived at her door at six the next morning, dressed in their most elegant attire, as if they were going to a wedding ceremony. Over seventy women and girls, ages 7 to 24, signed up to attend school that first day, from all of the surrounding villages. But some of the older girls dropped out when they learned that they would be taught by male teachers.

Mobilizing New Partners

After her school had been in operation for a year, Sadiqa's home was at the bursting point, with more than thirty girls in each class. Thanks to an anonymous donor who provided U.S.$13,000, she was able to add more classes, but still lacked an adequate facility for her students. She found support from an unexpected source – a nearby mosque – which offered her space for the school. "We read a lot of negative things about the mullahs here in Afghanistan," she says, "but many of them are pro-education, and we should work with them."

Over the next two years, Sadiqa and her associates at the Omid Learning Center would open three additional schools across Afghanistan, with one located in Wardak province (like the original school) and two in Nangarhār province, near the Pakistani border. Sadiqa has used her skills in persuasion to mobilize resources for her growing projects, relying on a range of friends and supportive organizations, including the Advocacy Project, based in Washington, D.C. While funding remains a key concern (two of the schools are run primarily out of tents located on barren land), Sadiqa's dream is becoming a reality. The Omid Center has recruited twenty-seven teachers, and today, nearly 1,100 Afghan girls who had never entered a classroom are attending school.

A soft-spoken, gentle young woman who wears the traditional scarf over her head, Sadiqa – despite her bright smile – is not immediately recognizable as the courageous and passionate advocate for girls' and women's rights that she has become. Jamila Afghani, an executive member of the Afghan Women's Network and director of the Noor Education Center for refugees, who has worked with Sadiqa for years, says, "She leads the community forward with smallness of means and greatness of purpose."

Sadiqa continues to manage the Omid Center, while seeking additional support both within the country and internationally. As much as she and so many of Afghanistan's women have already accomplished, Sadiqa still speaks of the barriers – both political and personal – that continue to keep women from taking leading roles in Afghan society. In early 2005, she spent a week in New York City at the United Nations, participating in an international women's conference – an experience that reinforced her resolve to fight for women's rights. Yet at home, her new husband, a young doctor, was constantly being questioned, sometimes harshly, about how he could allow his new bride to travel so far by herself.

Sadiqa says that she still draws great strength from her father, who has stood with her from the beginning. "When I fell, and didn't want to get up because I was so discouraged, my father didn't let me give up. He would tell me, 'If you fall, then learn why you fell down, because it will make you stronger.'" Sadiqa adds, "I feel so lucky to have such supportive people in my life."

It has been a long and at times difficult journey for Sadiqa, from a frightened young refugee fleeing her own country to a confident, articulate, and respected advocate for girls' education and women's rights. Yet at 25, she has barely begun. ∎

The Omid Learning Center, which Sadiqa founded in 2002, has recruited nearly thirty teachers and enrolled close to 1,100 girls in four schools across Afghanistan.

"With achievements more befitting an international CEO than a young woman, Sadiqa's positive mindset, fearless attitude, and energetic approach to life have resulted in remarkable feats. She knows that the greatest accomplishments require the greatest risks. With courage to dare, and the ability to bounce back from failure, I have no doubt that her success will continue, and her legacy will inspire."

Her Majesty Queen Rania Al-Abdullah
Amman, Jordan

ADVICE FROM SADIQA ON:

Preparing the Community for Change

- **Lay the groundwork.** Particularly when the program that you are trying to launch is a controversial one, in this case building girls' schools where such institutions had either been closed down for many years or never existed, it is important to raise awareness within the community and to prepare community members for change. Sadiqa called together parents and religious leaders from local villages to share her ideas and explain why girls' education was important. One unexpected ally was the local mosque, whose religious leaders saw what she was trying to accomplish and offered to help.

- **Build trust in the community.** "To start something new in any region of the world, it is always important to build trust among people," notes Sadiqa, underscoring the need for individuals to feel ownership of the program. "My intention is always to give people the sense that they own the project," she says, "so that they feel the responsibility, when the time comes, to take it over by themselves."

- **Establish a solid track record as part of your fund-raising strategy.** It is difficult to raise funds for a program that does not yet exist or that has not yet achieved its goals. Because Sadiqa was willing and able to use her own money to pay teachers, as well as use her own home to house the school, she was able to get the project off the ground. She then had a track record with which to raise funds for the school's expansion.

- **Respect the culture and don't move too fast.** Says Sadiqa: "In my country, it is necessary to respect the norms and culture of the society," even while you lay the groundwork for change. Also, moving slowly toward your goal is sometimes the best strategy. "Over the years," she warns, "Afghans have often raised objections against the government in power which has tried to constrain women. Steps taken too hastily forward, however, . . . have created resistance not only by religious groups and ultraconservative elements, but also from broad segments of the rural population."

SEINEP DYIKANBAEVA

Advocating for the rights of the disabled

KYRGYZSTAN

I have been dealing with the issues of disability since childhood, as I am a disabled person myself. Yet I believe that everyone, regardless of their physical condition, has the right to live a full life. Since my birth, I have wanted to be in society, to go to kindergarten, to university, and to work. I have lived, am living, and will live a full life, and for this reason, I want others not to give up and instead to try to achieve independence. The fact is, the disability isn't the obstacle. The real problem is poor public health services, discrimination, stigmatization, and the absence of resources. I do not feel my disability – I feel myself as a full member of society.

– Seinep Dyikanbaeva

Seinep, who suffers from infantile cerebral palsy, encourages other young people to stay active and not allow their disabilities to become a barrier to their independence.

Seinep Dyikanbaeva experienced a particularly traumatic start in life, barely surviving a long and difficult birth. Doctors predicted that she would probably not live; and if she did, she would be severely disabled. But Seinep survived, and while she lives with the very real challenge of a physical disability, she has become an inspiring role model to other disabled youth and their parents in her community, as well as a powerful advocate for the rights of the disabled through her work in a local nongovernmental organization.

Seinep, who grew up in the town of Bishkek in central Asia's Kyrgyzstan, suffers from infantile cerebral palsy, a chronic motor skills disorder that typically impairs leg and arm movement. While her family supported her efforts to lead an active and independent life, Seinep realized early on that the society around her offered few solutions and little or no assistance. Like many regions of the world, Kyrgyzstan provides very limited health and support services for the disabled, and negative stereotypes prevail. The government's financial support for disabled people is currently about U.S.$6 to U.S.$10 a month – far below the poverty line of U.S.$28. Parents of disabled children often can't find jobs because they need to dedicate so much time to caring for their children, and fathers sometimes abandon their families. Disabled children also face limited educational opportunities. Commonly denied regular schooling, they are forced into special schools or educated at home, unable to learn or socialize with their peers.

Mostly confined to a wheelchair, Seinep faces daily frustrations due to the lack of handicapped access to public buildings, including theaters, libraries, and schools. She also can't move around the city independently, as public transportation is not an option. "They do not stop for me," she says, "thinking that I am not able or won't pay." And when she initially applied to university, she was told she would be living on the third floor and would have to "adapt" to such conditions on her own.

From the beginning, Seinep's mother, Tamara, has struggled to care for her child while balancing the many other demands of work and family. Realizing there were no programs or organizations she could turn to for help, Tamara founded the Kyrgyz Association of Parents with Disabled Children (DCPA) in 1995, inspired largely by her daughter.

At the age of 5, Seinep had begun to talk about wanting to raise money to ensure that disabled children had the same opportunities as others. Her plan was to write poems and sell them. "If my daughter had these ideas and goals," recalls Tamara, "why couldn't I establish a foundation for disabled children and their parents?" Seinep was 10 years old when her mother decided to take action.

Seinep loves to express herself through music and poetry. Here she performs with her peers during an event honoring disabled youth.

Addressing the Needs of Parents and Their Children

Seinep was still in elementary school when her mother founded DCPA, but has since emerged as a powerful voice for disabled children in her community and a key leader within the association, where she serves as program coordinator and public relations manager.

DCPA's current staff of twenty volunteers works out of a three-room basement office in Bishkek. The organization aims to empower disabled children and their parents by ensuring that they have access to quality health, education, and other vital services. The association provides counseling, including psychological support, to parents and young people with special needs. Volunteers visit families, offering advice and working with them to resolve problems. DCPA also organizes activities for disabled children and their parents, including field trips, seminars, and special holiday events.

Over the past few years, DCPA has helped launch new services that support disabled children, including a rehabilitation center for forty disabled youth, and a small school that offers those with motor development delays a safe and supportive place to study. The organization also promotes the rights of disabled youth among media, government, and community agencies. While not a grant-making organization, DCPA helps individuals and groups access financial support for their activities.

Looking back, Seinep recalls how hard it was to launch DCPA. At the time, aside from two associations for the blind and deaf established during the Soviet era, no foundations dedicated to the needs of the disabled existed throughout all of central Asia. Residents in Seinep's neighborhood also resisted locating the association nearby. Reflecting a common negative stereotype, some local parents said they didn't want "sick" children to play with their "healthy ones." Many parents of disabled children were initially reluctant to join the organization, because it was the first of its kind and had not yet gained government support or encouragement.

Seinep acknowledges that there were other obstacles as well. She and her mother lacked basic management and fundraising skills. "Luckily, my mother and I were invited to seminars and conferences," says Seinep. While funding remains a challenge, DCPA is now supported by a range of national and international donors, including Counterpart International, Mercy Corps, Save the Children, and the Soros foundations network. Mobility International USA has also supported Seinep and her work, recruiting her for international seminars and workshops.

Working with Her Peers

Today Seinep's many responsibilities include evaluating the mental and physical conditions of the children who enroll in the program; counseling parents about the emotional and economic

Through her work at the Association of Parents with Disabled Children, Seinep helps to promote the rights of disabled youth.

DCPA also organizes activities for disabled children and their parents, including field trips, seminars, and special holiday events.

The staff at DCPA helps families to cope with the challenges of raising and caring for their disabled children.

challenges they face; and bringing families together to share experiences and lessons. Over the past few years, she has initiated a number of new programs at DCPA – including efforts to improve relationships between disabled children and their parents, and to encourage disabled youth to lead independent lives. Seinep's public relations work promotes her organization to the populace through the media and government agencies.

While Seinep is primarily confined to her wheelchair, she can walk short distances with assistance. Here, in a playful mood, she pretends to dance.

Seinep places a major emphasis on empowering her peers to lead more active lives – a focus that grew out of her own experience. Seinep admits that when she was younger, she looked to the state government to solve her problems. But thanks to her contacts with leading advocates in the disabled community, as well as her own determined spirit, Seinep has learned to be a "problem solver" herself.

"Those with special needs should be able to voice their problems and offer ideas and suggestions for how to solve them," she says. "If we don't start, who will do it for us?"

Changing Attitudes toward Disabilities

Seinep is particularly interested in changing young people's attitudes toward their disabilities. She feels she is very fortunate to have a family who supported her, and she wants to enable others to experience that same level of encouragement. "Thanks to my mother, I have achieved many victories and despite all, I have done a lot," she says. Proud that she attended a "comprehensive" (traditional) school, found a job at 18, and excelled in numerous competitions, Seinep feels she has taken control of her life. "I wanted to prove to all those who did not believe in my abilities and thought of me as 'disabled' that it is not true – so I try to destroy the stereotypes," she explains. "And thank God that is happening."

As a result of the many programs and training sessions provided by DCPA, Seinep believes there has been progress among her peers, who now see the positive side of life. "They now understand that their disability is not a final verdict – and that it is necessary to live a full life. Everything," she says, "depends on a person's attitude, and a disability is not an excuse to give up." As a result, more of her peers have enrolled in school and are active in their communities. Some have entered national and international cultural competitions and have been awarded prizes in both the arts and music.

Public attitudes toward those with disabilities seem to be shifting in a more positive direction, according to Seinep. As a result of the work of NGOs, she says, stereotypes are less common. Seinep is also pleased that these advocacy organizations are now banding together to create more of an impact. In addition, the mass media has started "to show the positive side of the lives of the disabled," she notes. "Society used to ignore us, but now the public's attitude is more to accept people with limited opportunities as equal members of society."

Focusing on Human Rights

DCPA recognizes that a broader movement is needed to secure the rights of those with special needs. "Why do I keep fighting for those rights?" Seinep ponders. "Because if there were no such rights, life would be even harder, and children wouldn't be able to protect themselves or struggle for equality." This, she says, would make them vulnerable and a burden on society.

Seinep, at 20, plans to go to a university to study sociology, human rights, journalism, and nonprofit work. Yet it is her continued optimism that she can overcome any obstacle that truly sets her apart. "I used to think that somebody else should help us," she says, "but now I understand that problems inspire us and direct our course in life." She also recognizes that her role as a leader and advocate is not always an easy one. "I understand that I am an example for some of our young members, which means I feel more responsibility about how I behave and cope with problems," Seinep explains. "That is why I try every day to be more positive, responsible, and trustworthy." ■

Seinep encourages her peers to be creative and to use their natural talents. The stuffed animal on her desk was made by a 13-year-old friend who suffers from a brain hernia.

"Human rights are the shared values of our world, but they need to be respected and implemented in practice worldwide. My current work has brought home to me the huge involvement of young people in tackling global inequities. They are at the heart of the global call for action on poverty, they support the small arms campaign, and they work at grassroots level on child rights, women's rights, combating stigma and discrimination in the context of HIV/AIDS, and working for peace and justice. These young people are the ambassadors of conscience who can renew our world."

Mary Robinson
Former President Ireland
Executive Director
Realizing Rights: The Ethical Globalization Initiative
New York, New York, United States

ADVICE FROM SEINEP ON:

Advocating for the Rights of a Minority Group

- **Draw on your own experience to teach others.** As a disabled person, Seinep is able to share her own experiences of the challenges of her physical disability with her peers, and thus more effectively mobilize them to lead independent and engaged lives. She knows both the difficulties and the possibilities of life, and is therefore a trusted voice who can inspire others.

- **Believe in your cause.** Because advocacy work can be exhausting and at times discouraging, it's important to believe deeply in what you are trying to accomplish. Seinep admits to being very discouraged at times, but she is always driven to continue her work because of her sense of responsibility toward others, and her deeply held belief that all children, regardless of their physical or mental conditions, have the same rights. She believes she has a "calling" for this advocacy work, and the "experience, knowledge, energy, ideas, and desire" to make a difference.

- **Network with like-minded organizations.** In the beginning, Seinep and her mother were very isolated because DCPA was the first organization of its kind in the region to address the needs of parents of children with disabilities. Eventually they were able to reach out to funding organizations and other foundations and nonprofits that share their commitment to improving the rights and conditions of disabled children.

- **If you don't have the skills to run an organization, learn from professionals.** Like many new organizations, DCPA was founded by individuals who felt passionately about their cause but had no experience in managing programs or raising money. Progress was slow until they began attending seminars and workshops on management, funding, and other essential skills.

- **Evaluate your program and keep supporters informed.** It is important to be able to demonstrate the impact that your organization is having on its beneficiaries as well as the larger community. DCPA, for example, carries out research and analysis of the challenges facing disabled youth, monitors and evaluates its programs, and keeps its funders informed of progress through regular reports.

HUGH EVANS

Rallying students to support the educational needs of children

AUSTRALIA

I think that young people today, whether in South Africa or Australia, want to do something about the world. The idealism of young people is fantastic. Some people say it's naïve, but if you are not idealistic you risk becoming hard-hearted. I believe we need a vision for our world of what we want it to be, of what it could be. Our world doesn't need to be the way it is but for our greed.

Those of us in countries like Australia are so fortunate. Our prosperity gives us incredible opportunities to be involved in creating a better world. All we have to do is dream and act on our dreams. The possibilities are as big as our hearts.

– Hugh Evans

Founded in 2003, the Oaktree Foundation is a movement of young people working to provide children and youth in the developing world with increased educational opportunities.

OUR TIME IS NOW

At 18, Hugh spent a year living and working in South Africa at God's Golden Acre, a home for HIV/AIDS orphans.

At the age of 14, Hugh Evans witnessed firsthand the devastating effects of poverty, particularly on children, during a two-week study tour of the Philippines. For several days, the Australian teen lived with a family in a slum community known as Smokey Mountain, a sprawling expanse of smoldering trash outside Manila, where thousands of families lived, scavenging for their survival.

On the first night of his stay, Hugh found himself sleeping next to a boy his age on a slab of concrete in a one-room hut. The boy lived with his family of seven in a space half the size of Hugh's bedroom at home in Melbourne. The experience left an indelible impression. "I didn't sleep a wink that night," he recalls. "The heat was oppressive. The stench of garbage from outside was overpowering, and there were cockroaches crawling all over me. With a new understanding of the severity of poverty, that night changed my outlook on life forever."

Hugh's experience in the Philippines was made possible by World Vision, a Christian relief and development organization that now works in more than one hundred countries to transform the lives of the poor. His involvement with World Vision had started more than a year earlier, when Hugh successfully raised more than AUS$1,000 during the organization's annual "40 Hour Famine"

campaign. Through the campaign, teenagers and others volunteer to go without food for a weekend and solicit sponsors to support their fight against global poverty.

Seeking to understand the root causes and effects of poverty would become a fascination for Hugh, an empathetic and altruistic risk-taker.

During high school, Hugh spent a semester on a study-abroad program in India, after which he volunteered for three weeks at refugee centers and orphanages in the country. At 18, when most of his friends were contemplating what to bring to college, Hugh once again set his sights overseas. "I wanted to get my hands dirty," he remembers. "I didn't want to end up after five years' study and a career looking back and saying, 'Man, what does my life count for?'" Deferring his university enrollment for a year, Hugh raised enough money to travel to a rural valley in the KwaZulu-Natal province of South Africa, a region hard hit by the HIV/AIDS crisis. There, with a grant from World Vision, he spent a year living at God's Golden Acre, a home for HIV/AIDS orphans, and overseeing the development of a community resource center and sports field. The experience, once again, proved to be transformative.

"Throughout my time at God's Golden Acre I felt a real sense of belonging," reflects Hugh, now 22. "I was an integral part of the everyday lives of the other volunteers and the children who lived there. Everyone knew my name and I knew everyone else's. By contrast, a sense of community connection seemed particularly hard for young people in Australia to achieve."

Hugh's deep concern for the children he encountered overseas, combined with his faith in God and commitment to being of service, prompted him to think: Why not engage other young Australians in a concerted effort to help their peers in poor countries?

In early 2003, Hugh mobilized a group of his fellow students to establish the Oaktree Foundation, a movement of young people seeking to provide children and youth in the developing world with educational opportunities and the chance to realize their potential. The organization's founders selected the oak tree as a symbol because just as an acorn matures into a mighty oak tree, so too can young people realize their full potential when given access to education and opportunities.

Nearly three years after its founding, Oaktree – one of the first youth-run development aid organizations in the world – has mobilized more than three thousand volunteers and supporters and established branches in five major cities in Australia (Melbourne, Sydney, Canberra, Brisbane, and Perth), as well as in Johannesburg and Durban, South Africa; Birmingham, England; and Boston in the United States. Through the collective efforts of these young people, the foundation has raised more than AUS$400,000 to support educational and community development projects benefiting young people in Australia, Ghana, the Philippines, and South Africa. Oaktree supporters include hundreds of individuals, as well as companies including Qantas Airways, Levi Strauss, J. Walter Thompson, and Toyota. In honor of his efforts, Hugh was recognized as the Young Australian of the Year in 2004.

So how did Oaktree grow from an idea into a national and, subsequently, an international initiative in less than three years? The answer lies in a well-thought-out plan for seeding its approach at schools and universities, and engaging the passion and creativity of hundreds of student volunteers.

Starting Out

During Oaktree's early days, members would meet at the home of Hugh's father, huddling around a coffee table in the living room. As the group expanded, they relocated, first to a room offered by their school, and next to a rented house. Today, Oaktree is headquartered in a formal office donated by one of its supporters. The office includes enough space for the foundation's four-member staff and fifteen team leaders, along with meeting room facilities.

Oaktree volunteers see education as being essential to helping young people realize their potential in life.

In honor of his efforts, Hugh was recognized as the Young Australian of the Year in 2004.

A major theme in Hugh's work – and life – is building community and nurturing global understanding among young people.

All of Oaktree's staff and the majority of Oaktree's board members are under the age of 26. In keeping with the organization's youth-focused charter, all accept that they will need to "retire" from their formal roles at their 26th birthday, with many continuing on as mentors and advisors. "I firmly believe that young people can change the world," affirms the tall, lanky Hugh. Yet even he admits that there have been times when he has questioned whether he possesses the knowledge and experience to guide and oversee a fast-growing organization. Currently finishing up a double-degree in law and science at Monash University, Hugh has grown accustomed to putting all of his reading off until just a few weeks before final exams.

Oaktree is structured much like its namesake. The organization's board of directors resembles the trunk of a tree, Hugh explains. The eight-member board charts the organization's growth and ensures that its various satellite operations receive the support they need to achieve Oaktree's mission. Chairing the board is a young lawyer, with other members offering expertise in business, finance, communications, and international development.

The staff is divided into various teams – technology, finance, legal, research, media and marketing,

advocacy, administration, and sponsorship – which represent the branches of the tree. These branches extend metaphorically into communities, where they plant the seeds (acorns) of Oaktree's growth at high schools and universities.

Oaktree representatives travel to various schools and give talks aimed at encouraging students to set up an Oaktree chapter of their own. Interested students receive a "seed pack" of materials, including a DVD, background information on the foundation, an explanation of volunteer responsibilities, and a step-by-step guidebook for orchestrating successful fundraising events. Past events range from art exhibitions to silent auctions, and from barbecues to movie nights. Proceeds support educational projects identified by Oaktree and its affiliated organizations in Africa and southeast Asia.

The heart of Oaktree's fundraising strategy is its "Dinners for Life," held annually during the last week of August. In 2005, the foundation seeks to mobilize 250 such dinners and special events at schools throughout Australia, South Africa, and select parts of the U.K. and U.S. Students organize events and invite their parents and other community members to attend. Funds raised from this year's Dinners for Life will be used to support the care of children orphaned as a result of the HIV/AIDS epidemic in South Africa, as well as an organization that provides educational and livelihood opportunities to young women recently released from ritual servitude in Ghana. While 2004's event netted AUS$100,000, Hugh hopes to generate AUS$250,000 in 2005.

Nurturing a Global Sense of Community

All of Oaktree's activities focus on nurturing connections and understanding among young people who are growing up in diverse contexts, yet share many of the same interests and dreams. To help young people better understand complex development issues, Oaktree has created educational modules that local chapters may use to stimulate discussion among students and participants at Oaktree events. In 2004, Hugh also wrote *Stone of the Mountain: The Hugh Evans Story*. In it, he tells of his experiences while living in South Africa and outlines a number of development lessons. Readers learn of the extent of the HIV/AIDS crisis in South Africa and the situation of AIDS orphans in the country; of the educational needs of children in the developing world; and of the importance of community-driven development, whereby members of a community each play a role in identifying and achieving shared goals.

In much the same way, Oaktree advocates that everyone, no matter where he or she lives, participate in building a fair, just, and sustainable global society. Says Hugh, "I believe the values that grow communities are the same values that nurture individuals – forgiveness, self-sacrifice, patience, compassion, and a desire to see justice in our society." ∎

Oaktree's fundraising efforts culminate every August with its "Dinners for Life" events.

"Hugh Evans's enthusiasm, passion, dedication, and ability to take on any challenge thrown his way epitomizes all we could hope for in the youth of our nation. It shines through in the way he inspires others to join him, the way he communicates so passionately, the personal interest he takes in people no matter where they hail from, and the respect he has for all who can teach him skills or give him pointers as to how to best use the privileged opportunities he has been given."

Tim Costello
Chief Executive Officer World Vision Australia
Melbourne, Australia

ADVICE FROM HUGH ON:

Initiating a Grassroots Fundraising Campaign

· **Seek powerful ways of telling your story.** When they conduct school visits, Oaktree members speak passionately about the organization's mission and the needs it seeks to address. Oaktree has developed several moving videos that schools may use in recruiting volunteers and engaging audiences during fundraising events.

· **Promote local ownership of the program.** Rather than prescribe specific events, Oaktree encourages participating schools to be creative. Past events have included scavenger hunts and comedy performances, black-tie dinners and bingo nights.

· **Ensure strict financial accountability in implementing fundraising campaigns.** Oaktree offers guidelines to local groups conducting fundraising, including how to obtain government licenses, tax deductibility requirements, and how monies are to be processed for the purposes of supporting Oaktree's development efforts.

· **Always say thank you.** Oaktree stresses the importance of both writing thank-you letters to all donors and publicly acknowledging their support.

Expanding a School-Based Initiative

· **Create a structure that can support the program's expansion.** Oaktree models its growth on the shape of an oak tree itself. Its board of directors and headquarters staff provide essential leadership and support to its affiliate operations in different locations.

· **Take care in developing user-friendly guidelines that each location can use in implementing the program.** Oaktree's *School Seeds Handbook* contains detailed information on the foundation and offers job descriptions for each person responsible for carrying out the program at the local level. This roadmap not only instructs local chapters how to carry out the program, but also ensures continuity.

· **Create systems to ensure quality control.** Oaktree creates a unified look and feel for its fundraising events through offering volunteer groups the use of its logo and multimedia materials. Local volunteers are asked to share any communications created using the Oaktree name and logo to ensure that the language is consistent with the organization's mission.

VIMLENDU JHA

Mobilizing citizens to save a river

INDIA

An organization of young people has its advantages and disadvantages. Most people think that wisdom comes with age, but we don't have any gray hair yet. Even so, we see ourselves as a strong people's organization. We definitely have gone beyond just being a campaign and are a recognized organization today. The Yamuna River and the environment are our immediate concerns, but the larger call is to get young people to participate in the community, and not just be fence-sitters. Struggles are many, but our spirits are high.

– Vimlendu Jha

Organizing voluntary cleanups of the Yamuna River, which becomes highly polluted as it flows past India's capital of Delhi, is a central focus of Vimlendu's youth-led organization.

"When I was a university student, I used to feel sick crossing that river," recalls Vimlendu Jha, referring to a highly polluted stretch of the Yamuna River that flows through India's capital of Delhi. "A river which was the source of life and livelihood for millions of people was now a neglected piece of existence." Protecting this remarkable river, which begins its 1,370-kilometer journey in the melting snows of the Himalayan Mountains and winds past the magnificent, white marble façade of the Taj Mahal, would become Vimlendu's passion.

Now a well-known environmental activist, Vimlendu works with government, media, community, and youth leaders to mobilize the public to actively promote a cleaner environment.

Today, the Yamuna River accounts for more than 70 percent of Delhi's water supply and is a critical source of irrigation for the surrounding rural areas. Yet even though more than fifty-seven million people depend on it for their livelihoods and survival, the river is an ecological disaster. As it meanders through Delhi, the river collects more than 50 percent of its pollutants – some two billion liters of chemical waste and untreated sewage a day – making it one of India's most endangered waterways. "Having to cross the river so often was a visible reminder of the ignorance that our civilization suffers from," Vimlendu says.

Five years ago, in 2000, Vimlendu turned his anger and frustration into action by launching a highly visible environmental campaign, which quickly evolved into an effective organization. "We for Yamuna" (now expanded into a larger effort dubbed "Swechha") has become a powerful voice in the community, advocating for greater awareness of the need to clean up the river, while mobilizing Delhi's citizens to become more actively engaged in conservation efforts. The group organizes community cleanups of the river, advocates for government policies to improve the environment, trains youth leaders, and has developed a curriculum for environmental studies for middle school students. "What's most integral to all our initiatives is the spirit of volunteering," notes Vimlendu.

Choosing an Unexpected Career

Now 25, Vimlendu continues to pursue his career as an outspoken environmental activist. Yet as is true of many youth leaders, he didn't set out to be a force for change in his community, nor did his parents approve of such an idea. Born into a lower-middle-class family in the state of Bihar in northeastern India, Vimlendu's father was a teacher whose dream was to see his son become an engineer, a highly prestigious profession in India. But Vimlendu rejected his father's wishes. Looking back, Vimlendu recalls witnessing a violent riot between the Hindus and Muslims in his town, and watching in horror as people killed each other in the name of religion. The memory of the conflict and other experiences of social injustice would dramatically influence Vimlendu's life choices.

"I knew I did not want to be an engineer, but I did not know what else to do. I had never heard of social work or NGOs [nongovernmental organizations]," Vimlendu confesses. As a student studying Sanskrit at St. Stephen's College in Delhi, he had his first taste of being active in social issues, joining antinuclear street protests and helping to raise money for victims of an earthquake. But still, his parents were not impressed. "They began to think that all of this activism was a waste," he says.

Less than a month after his "waking dream," Vimlendu and his colleagues launched "We for Yamuna."

Vimlendu remembers the moment that changed his life. On July 19, 2000, something snapped in him as he walked along the riverbank on the way to visit friends. About to graduate from university, he knew he had to make a decision as to the direction of his life. "I knew I wanted to do something useful," he explains. Of that day in July, he says, "I found the courage to heed my inner calling and decided to do something for this forgotten treasure – the Yamuna River. It wasn't a dream while I was sleeping, it was a dream I had while I was awake!"

As a first step, Vimlendu set out to learn everything he could about the river. He dove into research with a passion, spending his days reading books and articles in libraries and visiting scientific organizations. Recognizing that he could not accomplish much by working alone, he shared his newfound interest with his friends. Less than a month after his "waking dream," Vimlendu and his colleagues launched "We for Yamuna" – at first simply as a campaign to raise awareness of the river and the urgent need to clean it up.

Launching a Public Awareness Campaign

"As a group, we decided to concentrate on two primary things: one was the Yamuna River, and the second was volunteering," says Vimlendu. "We realized that we needed to build people's capacity to prevent environmental disasters from happening in the first place, rather than trying to 'cure' them in their aftermath." This work could be done, reasoned Vimlendu, only by encouraging the involvement of young people, who he believes are the future leaders of society.

Vimlendu urges young people to join in his anti-pollution campaign to protect the Yamuna River. The Taj Mahal, considered one of the eight wonders of the world, was built on the river's edge in the seventeenth century.

Acknowledging that the team first needed to raise public awareness and visibility for their cause, Vimlendu and his friends held meetings on environmental issues – with a focus on the river – in schools and colleges. They organized street plays,

Vimlendu raises public awareness about the need to improve the environment by organizing rallies such as this one, as well as public cleanups.

photo **exhibitions, film screenings, and workshops. And they mobilized people to take part in** *shramdaans* – **public cleanups. Soon the media began to take notice of the campaign's activities. "We received mass coverage in all the leading newspapers and television channels in the country,"** Vimlendu reports proudly. **The result, he** says, was increasing pressure on the government to act.

After persistent lobbying and media coverage of the emerging environmental movement, a chief minister of Delhi announced a five-day *shramdaan* – a voluntary cleanup of the river at eight different sites – and publicly acknowledged the work of We for Yamuna for the first time. As a result of the growing public pressure, the government became more involved in finding a solution to the environmental problems. City leaders invited Vimlendu and his associates to join others already working on a plan of action to save the river. Government officials also announced a multifaceted campaign to spread awareness about the river's polluted condition among Delhi residents, including a number of activities in the city's slums. At the request of We for Yamuna, for example, the city government put up fence grills on the river's overbridges to prevent people from throwing garbage into the water. The Supreme Court of India also directed the state government

to make Yamuna water "fit for consumption" by 2003. Since 2000, the government has invested substantial resources in programs to clean up the river, but according to Vimlendu, much more needs to be done.

At the request of We for Yamuna, the city government put up fence grills on the river's overbridges to prevent people from throwing garbage into the water.

Expanding the Mission

While We for Yamuna achieved considerable success in raising both its own visibility and public awareness about the river during its first year, Vimlendu and his colleagues still had not registered the group. They were worried that they were taking on too many overlapping concerns. As a result, in 2001 the young founders changed the name and mission of the organization to "Swechha – We for Change Foundation," retaining "We for Yamuna" as a prominent Swechha program. The Hindi word *swechha* means "by your freewill" – which better reflects the group's focus on mobilizing volunteers and creating a socially and environmentally responsible society.

A new mission, however, does not always translate into increased funding. Like many new organizations, Swechha suffered from lack of financial support. "We ran on spirit and not on funds," Vimlendu recalls. "For three years, I spent money from my own pocket, and along with volunteers even made paper bags to generate money [for the organization]." At times, he slept at the New Delhi railway stations because it was too late to return home after a long day of work.

Recognizing the need to ensure greater financial stability for his organization, Vimlendu decided to build up his own knowledge and skills. While still staying connected to Swechha's work, Vimlendu went back to school, receiving a master's degree in social work at the prestigious Tata Institute of Social Sciences in Mumbai. After graduation he joined Youthreach, a Delhi-based NGO, to head up their environmental program. After less than a year, however, he returned to Swechha, where he has served as director ever since. Because he receives no compensation for his work, Vimlendu takes on various consulting projects for governments and corporations, primarily around environmental issues, to support himself and further the work of his organization.

Today, Swechha has become a stronger, more stable organization, mobilizing more than a thousand volunteers and running on an annual budget of 30 lakhs (U.S.$66,000). Four full-time staff and ten key volunteers manage its many

activities from a cramped, one-room office on the terrace of the United Nations Volunteer (UNV) building in downtown Delhi.

Swechha has also broadened its scope of operations, reaching out to the government and community to raise awareness about environmental problems. Recognizing that public policies are critical for real progress to be made, Vimlendu is pushing for far greater transparency in how government funds are being spent and whether environmental cleanup programs are working effectively. Perhaps most importantly, he is trying to change the way public officials address the long-term problem of pollution. And he believes he is making some headway. "The government has started to realize that it is not just the infrastructure which will solve the problem. People need to start feeling that they own the river," he says.

Swechha publicizes the fact that some two billion liters of chemical waste and untreated sewage pollute the Yamuna River every day as it flows through the city of Delhi.

As a way to change people's relationship to the river and get them involved in its restoration, Vimlendu advances the idea that the river and those who live along its banks are quite literally "connected." Since 70 percent of Delhi's citizens drink water from the river, and 70 percent of the human body is made up of water, he explains, then "70 percent of each one of us is the Yamuna River itself."

Creating a New Generation of Activists

Says Vimlendu (here leading a protest to improve the environment): "We realized we needed to build people's capacity to prevent environmental disasters from happening in the first place."

Vimlendu has designed a curriculum called "Bridge the Gap," which is being implemented in four middle schools in Delhi.

Most of the organization's focus these days is on mobilizing young people to become part of the solution and not be "fence-sitters." For example, Vimlendu has designed a curriculum called "Bridge the Gap," which is being implemented in four middle schools in Delhi. The curriculum seeks to encourage volunteerism among young people, so that they can learn to "bridge the gap between man and nature, humankind and prosperity, need and want," explains Vimlendu. The course reaches about ten thousand students every year.

Swechha also mobilizes young people around pressing social and economic issues. When the December 2004 tsunami devastated part of south Asia, including coastal areas of India, the organization helped collect funds for relief efforts, organizing street theater and song festivals for the cause. More than fifty youth participated in the campaign. Believing that all citizens have something valuable to contribute to society, Vimlendu works with those who are marginalized in society, at one point organizing hundreds of handicapped youth to take part in a major river cleanup.

Perhaps the organization's most significant, long-term strategy for raising awareness about the Yamuna River is to train a new cadre of environmental activists. Toward that end, Vimlendu organizes two-week "Yamuna Yatras" – which take young people on learning tours up the river in part to introduce them to its original breathtaking beauty, but also to mobilize them to help end the pollution. For Vimlendu, it's a chance to demonstrate, firsthand, the river's journey "from purity to profanity." So far, Vimlendu has organized four of these leadership training boat trips, with more than a hundred youth participating.

In order to impact a wider audience, Vimlendu invites filmmakers, environmentalists, and development professionals to join him on these upriver expeditions and other educational activities. The organization released a film in June 2005, entitled *Jijivisha* ("the will to live"), which explores the relationship of the river to the people, livelihoods, and cultures it touches so deeply. Immediately generating much interest, it was screened before corporations, schools, government agencies, and the general public.

These days, Vimlendu's tall, striking figure is often seen along the banks of the Yamuna River, whether leading a community cleanup, guiding a youth group on a boat tour, giving an impassioned speech at a protest rally, or participating in one of his favorite activities – street plays. But he can also be found in the halls of government, in corporate headquarters, and in school classrooms, raising awareness about how the river plays a significant role not only in the region's economic and social well-being, but in its spiritual life as well.

One of the three most sacred rivers in India, and the subject of many ancient religious texts, the Yamuna is highly revered by Hindus as the place where Lord Krishna spent his childhood, playing his flute and dancing on the riverbank in the moonlight. Those who bathe in its waters, it is believed, will go to heaven and are morally cleansed of their sins. The Yamuna also flows past temples sacred to the followers of Buddhism, a fact that Vimlendu underscores in his efforts to persuade people across all ages, backgrounds, and beliefs to act responsibly.

Vimlendu readily acknowledges that there has not been sufficient progress in cleaning up and protecting this beloved river. But he is clearly hopeful about the future, knowing that every day, more and more young people are getting involved, as he did, in its revitalization. ■

One of the most effective ways that Vimlendu has found to advocate for environmental action is to organize two-week learning tours of the river for local youth leaders and the media.

"As the stories in this book demonstrate, young people are not simply the leaders of tomorrow, as adults love to say, but are potent leaders today. CIVICUS has had a long-standing commitment to promoting the role of young people in civil society organizations. We do so because the lens through which children and youth see the world is different from that of adults – and can generate improved social outcomes for current and future generations."

Kumi Naidoo
General Secretary and Chief Executive Officer CIVICUS
Johannesburg, South Africa

ADVICE FROM VIMLENDU ON:

Launching a Public Awareness Campaign

- **Research your issue.** When you decide on a course of action, it is important to find out as much as possible about the issue, in order to make the most persuasive arguments to the public. Even though Vimlendu knew he wanted to do something to clean up the Yamuna River, he admitted he was "completely clueless" about its history and how it became so polluted. He spent weeks in the library researching his new cause.

- **Use the media and other activities to spread your message.** We for Yamuna and Swechha tap the power of the media to gain public recognition for their work. Says Vimlendu: "Create news as well as noise." Also, use local activities, such as street theater, to reach and engage your audience.

- **Don't be afraid to speak against the status quo or put pressure on the government.** Even in its first year, the campaign was able to mobilize public pressure on the government to change its environmental policies through rallies and volunteer cleanups. More recently, educational trips up the river, involving journalists and policy makers, have also proved to be effective in mounting pressure on public officials to act.

- **Be as inclusive as possible.** "Don't consider any section of society to be unimportant; don't neglect anyone," advises Vimlendu. Also, do "cross learning" with other communities in order to help identify problems and discover solutions. "Keep bringing in fresh perspectives; the initiative should be boundary-less," he says.

- **Encourage others to take leadership.** Vimlendu underscores the need to encourage new leaders to emerge in the organization. "Build a second line of leadership," he advises, fully acknowledging that it's a difficult thing to do. It is also important to develop ways to ensure that the initiative is "owned" by the group, and not by an individual.

- **Document what you do.** Keep a record of your activities, challenges, and achievements. "It will help you, as well as coming generations," says Vimlendu.

JOCELYN LAND-MURPHY
& JESSICA LAX

Spreading a message of environmental sustainability

CANADA

Canadian youth have few positive young role models and are rarely shown reason to hope – let alone dream. They are bombarded daily by doomsday messages about the state of the world and the inevitability of a bleak future. We have learned that it is rare that youth are shown the power and opportunities they have today – every day! – to work towards their ideal world, to truly be the change they want to see. We came to realize not only the importance of providing genuine hope for a better future, but also of advocating specific, tangible, everyday actions individuals could take to build it.

– Jocelyn Land-Murphy

Promoting social and environmental justice lies at the heart of Otesha's work.

My work with the Otesha Project has given me more proof than I ever thought possible that change can, does, and will happen. I can now look back and see hundreds of moments where I witnessed a 'tipping point' right before my very eyes: a team member's dad trading in his SUV for a hybrid car; a group of students organizing to get fair-trade chocolate in their cafeteria; a group of kids running to tell us they'd biked to school that day; a young woman excitedly telling us how she'd been "letting the yellow mellow," rather than flushing the toilet. Looking at myself I can also see a very different person from the young woman who sat in despair almost three years ago. I hold the realization that there is nothing I would rather be doing, nothing that gives me more hope, than the work I am so privileged to do.

– Jessica Lax

OUR TIME IS NOW

The Otesha Project's goal: to reverse North America's unsustainable consumptive practices by empowering students to take action.

When they were both 21, Canadian university students Jocelyn Land-Murphy and Jessica Lax took a twelve-week trip to Africa that changed their lives – forever. The two met while traveling to Kenya with seventy other Canadian students as part of the Canadian Field Studies in Africa program, which offers students hands-on courses in everything from sustainable development to agro-forestry.

On their travels, Jessica and Jocelyn visited rural villages as well as sprawling urban slums, experiencing firsthand the devastating effects of poverty on families and, especially, children. In classes, they learned about the history of exploitation in Africa and the rest of the developing world, and they began to view their own lives in a dramatically different light.

Recalls Jessica, "As our trucks full of Canadian students pulled away from town after town – essentially dollar signs on wheels – people would try to climb up the sides to stick their crafts through the window for one more sale. They were risking their lives, but we had

already moved on to talking about the photos we took and the new camera lens we wanted, oblivious to the situation outside the window and, just like at home, to the world beyond our backyard."

During the trip and the days that followed, Jessica's emotions ranged from anger at those who would allow such inequities to take hold to guilt over her ignorance. In Jocelyn, she found a friend who shared her sense of outrage and desire to be part of the solution.

Shortly after their return home, the two launched the Otesha Project, which they had started brainstorming about while still in Kenya.

Translated from Kiswahili, a native language of Kenya, *otesha* means "reason to dream." The Otesha Project's goal: to reverse North America's unsustainable consumptive practices by empowering high school and college students to take action, particularly regarding their own consumer habits.

A close friendship underlies Jessica and Jocelyn's commitment to Otesha's work.

Through school visits, bike tours, theatrical performances, multimedia presentations, and other creative strategies, Otesha staff and volunteers advocate simple actions that both young and old alike can take to protect the planet's resources and ensure a more equitable, long-term future for its inhabitants. *Turn off the water when you brush your teeth. Take shorter showers. Buy used or sweatshop-free clothing. Switch to fair-trade coffee. Watch less TV and be wary of the influence of advertising on your values and behaviors.* In Otesha's view, all are small steps each of us can take to make our social and environmental impact more positive. Says Jessica, "Otesha's education programs focus on helping all of us reevaluate our daily choices to reflect the kind of future we'd like to see – rethinking what we really need, conserving resources, and voting with our dollars."

Over the past three years, the Otesha Project's message of environmental and social sustainability has reached more than thirty thousand students throughout Canada. Foundations, businesses, and government agencies have provided assistance, and Honda even loaned Otesha two hybrid cars for use as support vehicles during the group's 2005 Summer Bike Tours.

Asked what they feel is the secret to their success, Jessica and Jocelyn point to the creative strategies they use to motivate people to change their attitudes and behavior. Saving the planet, according to both, is not only serious work, but can also be fun.

Taking Otesha's Message on the Road

Their trip to Kenya was just the beginning of what would become an expansive journey for Jessica and Jocelyn. Upon returning home and launching Otesha, they decided to take their message across the country – by bike. For six months in 2003, the two, accompanied by thirty-one of their peers, traveled more than 5,500 miles from the west-coast city of Vancouver, British Columbia, to Corner Brook, Newfoundland, a small city in the easternmost part of the country. En route, the group gave presentations and performed sustainability skits at schools and community centers, reaching more than twelve thousand people with their message of individual responsibility. To this day, both girls are in awe of the warmth and generosity they encountered along the way.

"As we traveled across the country, the radiating energy of the Otesha team attracted everyone – from curious passers-by to grocery clerks," says Jessica. "Young people were attracted to our raw, idealistic but confident belief in a better world."

Both Jessica and Jocelyn exude an upbeat, can-do attitude. With a warm smile at the ready under her reddish-blond hair,

In Otesha's first year, Jessica and Jocelyn biked over 5,500 miles.

"Young people were attracted to our raw, idealistic but confident belief in a better world," says Jessica.

OUR TIME IS NOW

While on tour, team members take time to air dry their laundry and maintain their bikes.

The pair refer to themselves and their compatriots as "hopeful hooligans."

Jessica is known for her sensitivity to others, listening skills, and capacity for hugging. Jocelyn, always identifiable by her abundant, curly blond tresses, also combines warmth with commitment. As a teenager, she grew up feeling embarrassed by her parents' activist streak and "organic" lifestyle. Now, she says, she couldn't be more grateful for her mom's tofu and her dad's long hair.

The pair refer to themselves and their compatriots as "hopeful hooligans" who creatively question the status quo. Their lively imaginations and sense of humor are reflected in the theatrical presentation they developed that forms the basis for Otesha's community outreach. Delivered to high school audiences through Otesha's "Hopeful High School Hooligan" program, the twenty-five-minute "Morning Choices" skit explores how one's morning routine – from bathing and getting dressed to commuting to school – can impact the earth and all of its inhabitants. Featuring characters such as "Careless Consumer" and "Mother Earth," the play incorporates multimedia elements to demonstrate how actions in one part of the world can impact people living thousands of miles away. (For example, how buying an average cup of coffee in Canada can affect the environment in countries like Guatemala and contribute to worker exploitation. Or, on the other hand, how opting for fair-trade, organic, shade-grown coffee can directly contribute to positive change.)

Trained Otesha team members act out the skit, adapting its content to reflect local realities. Currently, eighty-six youth from eight Ontario high schools have received the training, which includes learning about issues related to sustainable consumption and how to engage the public in implementing solutions. These high school teams have already presented to more than five thousand of their peers.

In addition to carrying out year-round presentations in their local communities, Otesha team members continue the biking tradition initiated by the organization's founders. From April to October 2005, for example, one team of seventeen youth biked across the country, and three other groups of fifteen to twenty youth participated in two-month regional rides. Interested students apply to join the trips through the Otesha website (www.otesha.ca), and applicants come from as far away as Australia. Team members pay U.S.$4 a day to take part in the experience, with Otesha covering travel expenses for some students who can't afford the full cost.

While on the road, participants bike anywhere from twenty to one hundred kilometers a day, presenting at schools, camps, and community groups en route, while a support vehicle carries supplies and equipment. Each night, the group meets to review the next day's activities, their individual roles, and ways of tailoring their next presentation to the community they will be visiting. The experience proves deeply enriching for bike tour participants, who gain skills in teamwork, planning, consensus building, communicating to diverse audiences, and effective leadership.

Walking Your Talk

A visit to Otesha's headquarters, dubbed the "Hopeful Manor of Marvelous Mayhem," reinforces the organization's message of environmental sustainability. Located on the main floor of an eighty-year-old house in Ottawa, the office exudes a warm, homey feel. Jessica, Jocelyn, and four other staff members live and work here (the basement and second floor are staff living quarters), relishing the benefits of a communal lifestyle and short commute. Otesha's two-room office is decorated with an assortment of puppets the group uses in its presentations and "garbage art," such as a colorful, wall-mounted creature made from what was once a laundry soap container.

Tacked up everywhere are postcards that Otesha has received from across Canada and abroad, including one from well-known author Barbara Kingsolver, who wrote, "I cheer for all of you, and will keep spreading the passion we share as long as I can hold a pen." The group maintains a growing library of environmentally oriented magazines and books, including Daniel Quinn's *Ishmael* and Naomi Klein's *No Logo*. Callers are apt to hear music playing in the background, including one of Otesha's favorite groups, a socially conscious hip-hop band called Sweatshop Union.

With nineteen full- and part-time staff, the Otesha team holds as its mantra Gandhi's oft-quoted phrase, "Be the change you want to see in the world." Otesha's t-shirt designs are printed on garments that the group buys secondhand. The money that is saved is then donated to a nonprofit that provides alternative income to families of child-laborers, so that their children can attend school rather than work. Both Jessica and Jocelyn are vegans who purchase foods that are organic, local, and "low-packaged" to reduce the environmental impact caused by transporting food products long distances. Both bike everywhere they go, hang their laundry to dry, and make their own Christmas gifts. "Whatever we speak about is something we do," says Jessica.

Clever illustrations such as these appear throughout The Otesha Book.

Publishing *The Otesha Book*

Otesha advocates simple actions that each of us can take to preserve the environment.

In early 2005, Otesha proudly published its first book. Bound with two rings and sandwiched between covers created out of recycled cereal boxes, every copy of *The Otesha Book: From Junk to Funk* is custom-made. Prior to conducting a school talk, the group ships the cover materials and inserts for the book to the school's location, where audience members are invited to create their own copies. Divided into sections on water, clothing, the media, coffee, food, and transportation, the book presents a cornucopia of ideas for sustainable living. Introductory essays by Otesha staff offer accounts of how each became committed to a particular issue. Colorful illustrations, cartoons, and group exercises bring the book's content to life.

The Otesha Book makes patently clear the environmental and social consequences of current patterns of consumption.

The Otesha Book makes patently clear the environmental and social consequences of current patterns of consumption. For example, readers learn that the cotton used to make much of our clothing is the most heavily pesticide-sprayed crop in the world and that cotton growers and pickers are rarely paid fairly for their work. They also learn that today's culture of consumption is fueled by the roughly three thousand advertisements that the typical North American consumer sees each day. These facts, combined with clever illustrations and inspiring success stories, make the book both informative and inviting.

Sustaining Otesha's Work

After successfully completing their 2003 Bike Tour, both Jessica and Jocelyn could have counted up their successes and moved on. Yet both were so touched by the enthusiasm they experienced on the road that their commitment to Otesha's mission only grew. Fortunately, that commitment is now shared by a diverse pool of donors, including the Canadian government, Canadian and U.S. foundations, an outdoor equipment retailer, and

Be wary of the influence of advertising, cautions Otesha.

a soymilk manufacturer. Other companies make in-kind contributions of food, bike equipment, office supplies, translation services, printing, and graphic design work – to name only a few.

Appeals to funders are supported by the evidence Otesha collects about its impact on people's attitudes and behavior. At the end of each school presentation, student audiences are given post-cards on which they are asked to write an action they are committed to take in the subsequent week to help promote a more sustainable world. The students are urged to mail the postcard back once they have completed that action. Over the past year, more than a thousand people have written back. Those who complete the Otesha team training, as well as bike tour participants, also fill out evaluations to gauge their level of learning through the program, as well as their changes in lifestyle.

Rather than planning the evolution of their work five or ten years ahead, Jessica and Jocelyn prefer to focus on what they're currently doing so well – one year at a time. While admitting that today's environmental and social challenges are daunting, Otesha's founders recognize that hope lies in getting more people to truly recognize their role as global citizens with the power to create positive and lasting change. ■

"All around the world, young people often express dissatisfaction with society's apparently heedless destruction of the environment on which their future depends. We frequently hear their voices raised in protest against the seeming lack of action by their elders. Their dissatisfaction is also shown positively, such as through the promotion of creative new ideas for conserving the environment. Young people realize 'their time is now.' They are a major inspiration for environmental action throughout the world and a potent force for change. It is therefore essential that they are involved in environmental issues at all levels. This is something to which UNEP is wholeheartedly committed. We will continue to highlight the importance of engaging young people in all efforts to attain sustainable development, for their sake and for future generations."

Klaus Toepfer
Executive Director United Nations Environment Programme
Nairobi, Kenya

ADVICE FROM JESSICA & JOCELYN ON:

Starting an Advocacy Initiative from Scratch

- **Match your medium to your message.** Find a match between your message and the medium you use to get it across. By using bike tours and a play about morning rituals, Otesha emphasizes the choices people make every day.

- **Do your homework.** Jessica and Jocelyn carefully research environmental trends, seeking to understand all sides of issues. Neither had prior experience in fundraising, but they read "how-to" books and networked with countless individuals who were of great help.

- **Investigate in-kind sources of support.** Much of Otesha's work is made possible through the generosity of residents in bike tour destinations. "In addition to innumerable volunteer hours, people lend us their lawns to pitch tents on and hold potluck meals to keep us fed on tour," says Jessica. Otesha also receives a 50 percent discount on the rent of its office space.

- **Identify key allies.** Such allies can include friends and even family members. Jessica's parents have played an invaluable role in Otesha's work, including fine-tuning presentations, hosting retreats in their home, helping edit *The Otesha Book*, and troubleshooting obstacles.

- **Be persistent.** Don't be afraid to ask for what you want. While initially schools were reluctant to accept Otesha team visits, given the group's lack of experience and name recognition, Otesha staff kept on calling until a few schools eventually agreed to host them. Now, the group relies largely on word-of-mouth marketing to open doors at local schools.

Getting Your Message Across

- **Focus on positive solutions.** While Otesha is quick to point out the environmental ills befalling today's world, its message remains fundamentally upbeat. Its plays and publications stress positive actions each individual can take to create a more sustainable world.

- **Be creative. Make it fun.** Otesha uses humor in its skits, cartoons, and publications to communicate its message in a lighthearted, accessible way.

- **Walk your talk.** Otesha team members model the very behavior they advocate in their work. When its team members talk about individual responsibility, they do so based on their own personal experiences.

MARIA D'OVIDIO

Helping low-income families launch small businesses

ARGENTINA

I love what I do – giving opportunities and skills to other people, impacting their lives, and providing them with incomes. My whole purpose is to give them a chance to get to know themselves, and also become independent, and to change the way they see their roles in society. The hardest thing is to change the mentality of people who don't trust themselves or others. It means you have to spend a lot of time to build that trust with them . . . and it becomes a process of constant construction.

– Maria D'Ovidio

Intepay*

A micro-enterprise project, Intepay generates fair, safe, and gainful employment for women living in the slums of Buenos Aires.

As she enters a small, dimly lit candle factory in a poor Buenos Aires neighborhood, Maria D'Ovidio warmly hugs the three women workers who greet her. Pink, white, and red candles fill the shelves just above them, some of which will eventually be sold at upscale boutiques in New York City. The women talk excitedly about how the business is growing and about a new order that has just come in from a company that organizes large events. A casual visitor would have no way of knowing the many challenges these women have faced in getting this new enterprise off the ground – or how their lives have changed in the process.

Five years ago, Maria, now 27, was an at-times unsatisfied university student. The economics courses she took failed to address the root causes of the poverty and lack of opportunity that she saw around her every day. "I saw that something was missing in the theory," she explains. "I saw the trade-offs, who holds the power and who doesn't, and the huge inequities in income." One day, she attended a lecture given by Professor Muhammad Yunus, founder of the Grameen Bank in Bangladesh and a renowned leader of the global micro-credit movement. Listening to him talk about his book, *Toward a World without Poverty*, Maria learned that the Grameen Bank offers small loans to low-income people, primarily women, to begin their own businesses, "thus transforming a financial tool into a social tool."

Maria spent six months living in rural villages and studying how the Grameen Bank transformed the lives of poor women through the use of micro-credit.

Inspired by the idea that such a program could help close the ever-widening gap between rich and poor in Argentina, Maria persuaded her father to allow her to travel halfway around the world to Bangladesh. There she spent six months living in rural villages and studying how the Bank transformed the lives of poor women through the use of micro-credit. "The experience changed my life," she says, "and inspired me to come back to Buenos Aires, finish my college career, and see if I could do something the same."

Turning Theory into Practice

Upon her return from Bangladesh, Maria first helped to found Interrupcion, an organization led by young social entrepreneurs like her who wanted to make a difference. A nonprofit group that encompasses a growing number of projects, Interrupcion identifies, develops, and manages

As a university student, Maria did not believe her economics classes addressed the root causes of poverty that she saw around her.

socially responsible business ventures in the community. Its goal: to "interrupt" the ongoing economic system that dehumanizes the poor and instead add value and dignity to people's lives.

The founding members of Interrupcion each began to develop their own initiatives, and in 2002, Maria launched her personal micro-enterprise project. She named it Intepay – a combination of the traditional Quechua words for sun (*inti*) and father of light (*pay*). Over the three intervening years, Maria has worked (currently with a staff of four) to create small enterprises that are now helping some of the city's poorest inhabitants to climb out of poverty. The candle-making project was the first and, so far, is the largest of these enterprises; but the Intepay projects in four Buenos Aires slum neighborhoods have also helped low-income men and women to start new businesses sewing clothes, knitting, and silk screening designs on shirts and other apparel.

Maria is slowly transforming public perceptions of what impoverished citizens are capable of achieving.

A recent economic crisis in Argentina has translated into untold hardships for many of its citizens, with nearly half living below the poverty line, many of them unemployed. The average annual income in the country is U.S.$12,000. The depressed economy, while improving, reinforces the urgency of Maria's work. "This is not only an alternative way of employing vulnerable populations," she explains. "It's rebuilding social capital in the poorest communities." By working with families to produce goods and services that are competitive within the local marketplace, Intepay seeks to restore people's sense of dignity and the value of their work, and thus impact the community and its families on a broader scale.

Today, Maria's programs directly affect 150 people and indirectly benefit another 300. In the process, Maria is slowly transforming public perceptions of what impoverished citizens are capable of achieving.

Launching a Candle-Making Business

Judit, Adriana, and Laura were all living in one of the poorest neighborhoods in Buenos Aires, but they didn't meet until they came together as trainees in Maria's candle-making project. "In the beginning, we thought we couldn't do this," says Laura, a 33-year-old mother of four.

Maria joins Judit, Adriana, and Laura in their candle-making workshop. Taken together, Intepay's micro-credit projects directly impact 150 people and indirectly benefit 300.

Candles from the Intepay project are sold to event-planning groups in Buenos Aires and in shops in New York City.

Intepay produces high-quality merchandise, such as these candles, while providing marketing and management skills to the men and women who create them.

Laura and her coworkers hoped that this training would help them earn some much-needed income. While one of them had worked before, as a housecleaner, the others had never found a job. Today, they have learned to work together as a team, and in total they produce as many as one hundred candles an hour. All three help manage the production and sale of their products, and, increasingly, they work directly with their clients – an aspect of the business that Maria previously handled.

After a slow start, the project is finally making a profit. Each woman earns about 250 to 600 pesos (the equivalent of roughly U.S.$100) monthly above the 1,300 pesos a month they jointly spend on materials, gas, electricity, and water. And business is growing. Just recently the business received two contracts to produce four thousand candles for large clients. Improvements in the work area are also being made. Judit, Adriana, and Laura have painted the somewhat dark and cavernous room where they work, and a local company has donated money to install a new bathroom.

Starting Out: Developing Key Allies

Maria's red-tinted hair, high boots, and boundless energy reflect a truly dynamic personality. Talking with her is like sipping an espresso. She warms you up with her quick smile and rolling laughter, and energizes you with her ideas. Words sometimes tumble out of her mouth so fast that it is difficult to keep up. While she's been known to dance all night, she pursues her work and ongoing studies with tireless passion.

One of the primary strategies for developing her micro-enterprise project is to create alliances with community-based organizations. When she launched the candle-making project in Buenos Aires' Doc Sud neighborhood, Maria worked closely with local community groups to help recruit participants. The candle-making project operates out of a formerly deserted building that was donated by a community center located next door. Some of the children of the candle-makers spend time after school at the center, which offers educational and recreational programs.

A number of local businesswomen donate their time to teach budget and management skills to the new entrepreneurs in Maria's projects.

Mobilizing financial and other support from outside organizations and individuals, particularly those who are willing to give in-kind contributions, has been critical. For example, a number of local businesswomen donate their time to teach budget and management skills to the new entrepreneurs in Maria's projects, and a leading artist in Buenos Aires works with women in the candle-making project to help them design their products. Maria's organization has developed an impressive board of directors – including a bank vice president, an economist, and several government and community leaders – who provide critical support and resources.

"We want to develop people's skills – in terms of management and leadership," explains Maria.

While Intepay provided the first project – the candle-making factory – with a start-up grant of approximately U.S.$300, the group offered the subsequent projects, such as the clothing initiatives, long-term, no-interest loans of U.S.$4,000. To facilitate repayment, a social fund has been established. About 15 percent of a project's earnings go back into the fund of each Intepay enterprise, which accumulates until participants can pay back the original loan.

Focusing on Empowerment

Over the years, Maria, who still spends some of her time in the Interrupcion office and draws inspiration from her colleagues, has provided micro-enterprise participants with the knowledge and experience to run and manage their own businesses. "We want to develop people's skills – in terms of management and leadership," she explains. "It's really about self-development – making sure they own the ideas and manage their own resources." In the long term, the aim is social empowerment, Maria says, "where we're building people's capacity to live independently and with dignity." She adds: "Eventually, you want to change how they see their roles in society – as mothers, workers, and citizens in their communities." Training sessions stress participatory democracy, respect for others, leadership development, and goal setting. The objective of the Social Empowerment Team, says Maria, is to ensure that the entrepreneurs have not only the ability to organize and manage their micro-enterprise but also the skills and confidence to develop a plan for the future.

Vincent, 58, at first found it a challenge to learn how to sew, but he is now pleased to be making a small profit in his new business.

The women involved in the candle-making project reflect this growing sense of confidence and purpose. In addition to the much-needed income, these entrepreneurs discovered an unexpected pleasure in working together, getting out of the house, and finding a new community. But ultimately, the impact on their lives has gone even deeper. "I never thought I could do something of value," says Judit, age 46. "Now I know I can. Learning all the new things all the time is exciting." This newfound confidence has also enabled Judit to get out of an abusive relationship. "Her husband was beating her," explains Maria. "Now she has this new income, and her husband has moved out. She started valuing herself."

It hasn't always been easy. "The hardest thing to change is the mentality of people who don't trust themselves or others," Maria cautions. "It means you have to constantly work to build that trust with them."

Growing the Micro-Enterprise Model

The expansion of Maria's micro-credit model into other areas has been recent. Acquisition of four sewing machines has enabled her to develop the clothes-making business, as well as the small enterprise that stamps designs on clothing. Participants take an intensive, six-month training course, and the clothing project is about half a year away from breaking even. In the coming months, Maria hopes to expand the business by selling the products through local cooperatives, weekend open-air markets, and some individual

clients in the Buenos Aires area. Reflecting the poverty level of her new entrepreneurs, four of the clothing-makers live in a nearby abandoned building where there is no security, no glass in the windows, and no working elevators. But this new job has changed their outlook. As one of them said, "I didn't imagine I could do this, and now I feel I've achieved something. Now I want to be part of a big enterprise and work harder every day."

"The hardest thing to change is the mentality of people who don't trust themselves or others," Maria cautions.

While she continues to develop new micro-credit projects, Maria has even more ambitious plans. She is currently collaborating with colleagues from the academic, private, and public sectors to open a site where small businesses can be nurtured before they are launched – as a way to expand the number of micro-enterprises and ensure their sustainability. "I've been working on this for a year," Maria says excitedly, "trying to integrate talented people from the university, government, and private corporations." Her long-term goal is to collaborate with the government to reach three million low-income people across Argentina through her social enterprise model.

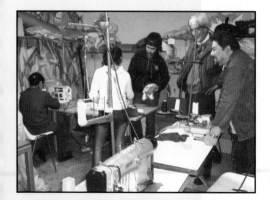

In addition to the candle-making factory and a sewing project, pictured here, Intepay has expanded its micro-enterprise work into clothes design.

Working long hours over the past four years has been a draining experience. But Maria refuses to let up in her fast-paced life. "I am inspired every day by making change possible and engaging others in these activities," she says. "They don't think they can do it, and we can show them these opportunities. With each action, we aim to show them: If you work hard, and have the tools, you can make things work. You can do it." ■

Maria's project is aimed at not only moving people out of poverty, but also ensuring they gain the skills and confidence to find dignity in their lives.

"In nations around the world, young people not only play valuable roles in stimulating economic revitalization but are at the heart of efforts to build more democratic societies. Through her innovative work in promoting micro-enterprise projects in impoverished neighborhoods in Buenos Aires, Maria D'Ovidio is accomplishing both – providing skills and employment to help people climb out of poverty and also the self-confidence to shape their own futures. It is in the best interest of the business community to look for ways it can creatively collaborate with youth in achieving the goal of poverty alleviation through wealth and job creation."

Maria Livanos Cattaui
Former Secretary General International Chamber of Commerce
Switzerland

"Maria is an amazing young woman, a marvelous example of what can be accomplished when a young person has a passion for change, the motivation and dedication to persevere, and the natural skills to make it happen. Her Intepay project reflects her vision that citizens of all ages should have the skills and support to lead dignified and empowered lives. She is part of a global movement of youth leaders who are developing long-term solutions to the challenges facing their communities."

Rick Little
President and CEO ImagineNations Group
Founder International Youth Foundation
Pasadena, Maryland, United States

ADVICE FROM MARIA ON:

Starting a Micro-Enterprise

- **Create strong alliances with existing organizations.** When starting out, it is important to work with community groups who have established networks. Explains Maria: "Local NGOs are already involved with the people, so they know their needs and challenges. It's important to build good relations with them."

- **Adhere to your long-term goals.** Maria says that her goal is not only to expand the number of people who are employed. Participants must "own" the project and lead all aspects of the enterprise. Helping individuals to find dignity and confidence in their work is the ultimate goal.

- **Provide a range of training opportunities.** A successful micro-enterprise model must deliver practical training – how to produce a product – as well as intensive training in management, budgeting, and leadership.

- **Set up a practical system for paying back loans.** Intepay created a social fund in which a small percentage of the enterprise's profits go back into the fund of each project. As the fund accumulates, the loan can be paid back over time.

- **Recognize that such projects take time to develop.** It takes time to recruit participants, establish a team, and build people's capacity to produce a product and manage its distribution.

Developing Partnerships

- **Mobilize support through in-kind contributions.** Intepay draws on the talents and resources of artists, local business leaders, and others who donate their time to work with and train new entrepreneurs.

- **Link up with people from every sector of society to promote your project.** Says Maria: "I work with consumers, workers, corporations, clients, and universities. They all speak different languages, but our message is the same – to empower people." Maria also says that it is easier to collaborate with others who are driven by the same ideas, "so you can solve problems together."

- **Create a strong board of directors.** Strive to achieve a diverse membership with representatives from the public, private, and nonprofit sectors. You will need them all.

RAMZI ABUREDWAN

Healing through music

PALESTINE

Arnaud Brunet/Gamma

Music is the universal language that everybody all over the world can understand. It is above words, so when human links are broken, music can be a bridge, bringing together people of every tribe and every age. Music is also a powerful force for tolerance and openness in the world. The cultural exchanges that music offers will help bring about greater understanding of others. For me, music gives sense to my life.

– Ramzi Aburedwan

Through the work of Al Kamandjâti, hundreds of Palestinian youth living in refugee camps are learning how to play a musical instrument.

Arnaud Brunet/Gamma

Ramzi, here helping one of his students to hold a violin correctly, teaches young people in the West Bank to play both Western and Arabic music.

The sound of laughter fills the air of a small classroom as roughly twenty children gather around their music teachers. Located in a community center in the Al Amari refugee camp near Ramallah on the Palestinian West Bank, the classroom is one of the few places where young people growing up in this impoverished neighborhood can come together and enjoy themselves. Twenty-five-year-old Ramzi Aburedwan, one of the instructors, bends his tall, thin body over a young boy, carefully demonstrating how to hold a violin. A patient teacher, he is passionate about music and eager to share that love with his new student.

Nearly seventeen years ago, when Ramzi was 8, the same age as the boy he now teaches, the scene was very different. Instead of holding a musical instrument, Ramzi clutched stones in his small hands, overcome with rage and utter helplessness. He had been walking home from school with his best friend, arguing over whose house they would visit to finish their homework. All of a sudden, Ramzi's friend collapsed beside him. "I saw a bullet wound in his head and blood coming down," says Ramzi, recalling that terrifying day and the sight of Israeli soldiers standing nearby.

Ramzi grew up in the Al Amari camp, where his family had lived for decades. Life was a daily struggle in his poor, isolated neighborhood. The increasingly violent resistance by some Palestinians against the Israeli occupation of Palestinian territories was a fact of daily life. The occupation that resulted from Israel's victory in the war of 1967 led to the Palestinian quest for their own independent state. A 1987 uprising against the occupation, called the First Intifada, raised the level of violence on both sides.

With the sudden death of his friend by a stray bullet, Ramzi, a second grader, was pulled into this escalating conflict. He remembers, "I was a kid, and I did not understand why they did that to my friend. I was in shock." He began to run toward the Israeli soldiers, picking up stones and throwing them as hard as he could. Over the next few years, Ramzi would express his anger at the loss of his friend in the only way he knew how – by continuing to throw rocks at the Israeli soldiers who were often stationed near the refugee camp. He admits his grandfather would sometimes tie him to his bed, terrified that one day, his grandson might not return home.

Transforming Anger into a Life of Music

Today, Ramzi is an internationally renowned musician who reaches thousands of people through concerts that he performs across Europe, the

United States, and Palestine. He is also founder and president of the nonprofit Al Kamandjâti association (www.alkamandjati.com), which runs music-training workshops for Palestinian youth from refugee camps in the West Bank and Gaza. Recognizing that children are early victims of violent conflicts, Ramzi has become a strong voice advocating for the universal right of all children – including Palestinians – to attend school, express themselves, and live in peace.

Realizing his dream to teach music to Palestinian youth took years. It began the day Ramzi, at 17, met Muhammad Faddel, a music teacher who introduced him to a number of instruments. It was the viola that captured Ramzi's heart. "I was so emotional hearing these new sounds, and being able to touch this musical instrument," he remembers. Clearly talented, Ramzi began to attend the National Conservatory of Music in Ramallah. His life and plans for the future soon changed dramatically.

Following his newfound passion, Ramzi would visit a music camp in the United States and then spend the next seven years in the French town of Angers, about two hundred miles southwest of Paris. There, on full scholarship, he studied at a music conservatory with students from many countries. Yet as his love of music grew, so did his determination to share the joy that music brought him with Palestinian youth living in the refugee camps. Quite simply, he wanted to replace the sound of violence with the sound of music.

Communicating a Message of Hope and Tolerance

Ramzi founded Al Kamandjâti in October 2002, while he was still a student in France. The organization, whose name translated from Arabic means "the violinist," aims to promote music education among Palestinian youth and strengthen their appreciation for Palestinian culture and identity. "I want people to know that I came from a refugee camp and that we are like all other kids in the world – even though our resources are limited," Ramzi explains. "I feel that I have to reach children with this message so they won't live without hope."

After raising seed money for the organization through concerts and public lectures and developing an academic framework and model music lessons, Ramzi and six members of the association traveled from France to Palestine to begin teaching children living in refugee camps. The new volunteers, many of whom were Ramzi's fellow music students from Europe and the United States, also began to perform public concerts in the West Bank and Gaza. The following year, in August 2003, more than three thousand Palestinian children participated in the music training workshops organized by Al Kamandjâti. "These programs give them a chance to show the community and the rest of the world what it means to be a Palestinian, and to aspire to a better future," Ramzi says.

Ramzi believes that all young people have the right to play games and express themselves creatively. Through its music lessons and public concerts, Al Kamandjâti is working to expand those opportunities.

Reflecting his appreciation for different cultural traditions, Ramzi teaches and plays both Western classical music, such as the works of Brahms, Bach, and Mozart, and the music of Arabic composers, including Oum Kalsoum, a popular singer whom Ramzi remembers hearing on the radio when he was growing up.

Arnaud Brunet/Gamma

According to Nellie Epinat, a French singer who works with Al Kamandjâti, the organization emphasizes "the importance of music as an alternative means to finding peace within oneself and with others."

Ramzi's work is inspired in part by his own refugee camp experience and his knowledge of the difficulties faced by young people who have few safe places to get together and even fewer opportunities to play games or sports. "When you take the hand of a child and introduce him to a musical instrument, then perhaps you can keep him from throwing stones," Ramzi says. "By doing this, you also recognize the rights of children to engage in play and recreational activities appropriate to their age, and to participate freely in the cultural life of their community."

Establishing Cultural Roots in the Community

The association's music program for young people has gained growing support within the Palestinian community. Recently, Al Kamandjâti opened up a music and cultural center in Ramallah that features rehearsal areas and a large hall for concerts. It offers two hundred children musical "awakening"

lessons, while providing older youth with direct music instruction in violin, viola, flute, double bass, and singing. A second music center is being renovated to accommodate the growing number of music and cultural activities being supported by Al Kamandjâti. Ramzi is pleased that through these activities, refugee children are finally gaining access to educational opportunities that until now had been the privilege of only a few. Says Ziad Khalaf, the executive director of the A.M. Qattan Foundation (a local Palestinian organization), "He is reaching out to Palestinian youth to help them realize their creative potential."

Quite simply, Ramzi wanted to replace the sound of violence with the sound of music.

Ramzi is committed to expanding the music teaching program, which is currently serving refugee camps in the West Bank, Gaza, and Lebanon. In the future, Al Kamandjâti plans to branch out beyond music workshops and concerts to form youth choirs and youth-led orchestras. Its long-term strategy is to integrate these music classes into local school systems. "We are obliged," says Ramzi, "to give children living in the refugee camps the same possibilities as any other children."

Today, Al Kamandjâti is headquartered in a small office in Angers, where a staff of up to fifteen volunteers runs the organization's far-flung activities. About 150 active members volunteer to organize the artists' trips and help raise funds to sustain the music schools, some of them working permanently in Palestine.

Balancing Words and Actions

While the work of Ramzi and his colleagues clearly provides direct benefits to the young people who participate in the music workshops, Al Kamandjâti also promotes a broader message of peace through nonviolence. Explains Nellie Epinat, a French singer living in Belgium who has accompanied Ramzi on trips to Palestine, "They do a tremendous job of [raising] public awareness around the situation of the Palestinian people and the importance of music as an alternative means to finding peace, within oneself and with others." She also says that Al Kamandjâti serves as a bridge, "not only between two countries, but between two different worlds, two societies, two cultures." Ramzi recognizes this larger context of his work, and although he has accepted a teaching position at the Edward Said National Conservatory of Music in Ramallah, he will continue to volunteer in the Al Kamandjâti music schools. Artists, he says, have a particular responsibility to promote social change. "But everyone can make a difference." ∎

Arnaud Brunet/Gamma

Arnaud Brunet/Gamma

Musicians from all over the world join Al Kamandjâti in providing educational and musical events across the West Bank and Gaza.

"As a Palestinian refugee, Ramzi found his sanctuary in the universal expression of human creativity – music. As a victim of both dispossession and occupation, he triumphed over his oppression to claim that spiritual victory of a boundless imagination. Instead of succumbing to his pain and captivity, he succeeded in generating a space of freedom not just for himself but also for those who, like him, are captives of history. Such is the gentle nature of genuine power."

Hanan Ashrawi, Ph.D.
Secretary General Palestinian Initiative for the Promotion of Global Dialogue and Democracy – MIFTAH
Member Palestinian Legislative Council
Ramallah, Palestine

"Today, Ramzi is no longer a street fighter but has become an internationally recognized musician. His story, to me, symbolizes the possibility of transformation: from militant opposition to creative spirit. He embodies hope and displays the kind of positive energy that could provide essential building blocks, not only for his own artistic career, but for a future Palestinian state."

John Marks
President Search for Common Ground
Washington, D.C., United States

Arnaud Brunet/Gamma

ADVICE FROM RAMZI ON:

Using Art as an Instrument of Social Change

- **Focus on the form of artistic self-expression you enjoy most.**
  Music emerged as Ramzi's passion early in life. That passion comes
  through every time he gives a concert, teaches a child, or approaches
  a potential sponsor. Says Ramzi, "With music, you create a future
  and peace of mind; it makes you smile."

- **Identify the audience you want to reach.** Ramzi's early childhood
  experiences impressed upon him the importance of reaching children
  with a message of peace and hope before violent attitudes become
  too deeply ingrained. In his view, music offers young people an
  alternative form of expression. Through its concerts, Al Kamandjâti's
  reach extends these positive messages to the general public.

- **Use your art to transmit a positive message.** Art is a powerful
  tool for change. Says Ramzi, "Artists and musicians must use their
  wide access to the public to transmit a message that can change
  people's minds. . . . It is both our duty and responsibility to be
  socially committed."

- **Be creative in how you blend your art with your
  commitment to social change.** Consider what
  messages you are trying to get across and the themes
  you want to weave through your artistic expressions.
  Ramzi is careful to blend the music of different cultures,
  emphasizing the importance of honoring diverse musical
  traditions. As another way to stress tolerance and
  understanding, he also recruits musicians from all over
  the world to participate in his concerts and workshops.

- **Use the art you create to generate income for your
  activities.** Musical performances generated funding to
  get Al Kamandjâti off the ground, and they continue to
  provide critical financial support for the organization. If
  you are teaching young people to paint or draw, hold
  an exhibition of their work, or get well-known artists to
  donate their art for a benefit auction.

For further information, visit: **www.alkamandjati.cc**

ERION VELIAJ

Promoting active political participation

ALBANIA

We thought that it is about time for all Albanians who want their society to grow and develop to say, 'Enough! I will no longer accept this situation! Enough with the corruption, poverty, and ignorance that are taking over this country! Enough with violence, trafficking, pollution, and backward and undignified politics! Enough with the poor water and electricity supply!'

Now that we said 'enough,' will these suffice? Of course not. The campaign aims at encouraging a spirit of civic revolt, sparking a sense of community, and increasing pressure on the policy-makers. This requires serious commitment from all citizens, a movement where everyone makes a sincere effort to get involved. . . . If the popular demand for change does not grow, then we can be assured that every government, this one and the ones to come, will not bother to offer more.

– Erion Veliaj

MJAFT!'s logo is a well-recognized symbol of protest and positive change in Albania.

Like many great ideas, the vision behind MJAFT! – a youth-led social justice movement in Albania – was conceived in a coffee shop. It was on a cold day in December 2002 that Erion Veliaj, then 22, and two high school friends, Arbjan Mazniku and Endri Fuga, took refuge in a neighborhood café in Tirana. Their conversation, as it often did, quickly turned to Albanian politics and what was wrong with their country.

MJAFT! seeks to creatively engage Albanian citizens in debating and taking action around issues they care about.

"We asked ourselves, 'Why do I belong to a system I can't change?'" recalls Erion. Only this time, their talk turned to what they might do to improve the situation. Citing many of the problems in their country – pollution, unemployment, corruption, and poor-quality education, to name only a few – the group finally identified what they considered to be the most vexing challenge of all: apathy.

"Everyone was waiting for a miracle to happen," says Erion. "They were bitching, but nobody was doing anything. Symbolically, it's like people signed a certificate of silence." Erion explains that Albanians tend to blame their situation on the nation's communist past and legacy of being taken over by outside forces, adding, "But when you're young, you can't live your life by blaming the past."

Instead of dwelling on problems, he and his friends started looking at solutions. Together, they conceived of a plan to awaken the nation's citizens from a century-long nap. Four months later, MJAFT! emerged as a potent social justice campaign aimed at stimulating citizen action and debate on urgent social issues. Over its first two years, MJAFT! evolved into a nationwide movement that today boasts more than ten thousand members – both young and old alike.

Translated from Albanian, *mjaft* means "enough." The campaign's striking logo, a red hand on a black background, borrows the colors of the Albanian flag and has become a nationally recognized symbol of citizen empowerment.

Employing a variety of creative, awareness-raising strategies, MJAFT! campaigns have been credited with the ouster of unpopular public figures, increases in the national education budget, new laws prohibiting discrimination against Albanian immigrants abroad, the reduction of telephone and electricity tariffs, and bans against the importation of genetically modified foods and unclassified waste. MJAFT!'s innovative tactics have earned it a growing reputation throughout the region and beyond, with youth activists from as far away as Zimbabwe and Iraq seeking to learn from its approach. Prominent universities in the U.S., including Harvard, Columbia, Georgetown, and New York University, have invited MJAFT!

representatives to share their experiences in promoting greater citizen participation and democratic reform with student audiences hungry for practical, real-life examples.

How does MJAFT! manage to institute change where others' efforts end only in talk? While Erion asserts that "there is no magic formula," he attributes MJAFT!'s success to a combination of timing, personalities, and even the availability of technological innovations like cell phones that facilitate fast, far-reaching, and cheap communication.

What prompted him to return was the knowledge that if his generation didn't take action, nothing would ever change.

Giving Back: Where Did It All Begin?

While frustration with the status quo in Albania served as a prime motivator for Erion, the seeds of his activist zeal were sown much earlier. After the death of his father when Erion was just 11, he learned the value of hard work and how to be self-sufficient. From his mother, he came to appreciate the importance of kindness and generosity. Erion's first voluntary activity began as a teenager, when he initiated a mentoring program for children in Albanian orphanages, raising money from U.S. donors, particularly in the state of Tennessee, where he was dubbed an honorary citizen.

After completing high school, Erion took advantage of a chance to study in the United States, his college years frequently interrupted with assignments for relief organizations. Initially he worked in refugee camps in Kosovo. Later he served as a crisis management consultant in parts of East Africa and Latin America. By the age of 22, he had spent time in roughly sixty of the poorest and most conflict-ridden countries of the world.

Erion confers with Edi Rama, Tirana's mayor, during a MJAFT!-organized event.

Like many smart, talented youth from the Balkans, Erion admits that he could have forsaken his native land to pursue opportunities elsewhere. What prompted him to return was the knowledge that if his generation didn't take action, nothing would ever change. "We have to stick around and make this place work," he emphasizes. Today, he devotes up to eighty hours each week to his work as MJAFT!'s executive director, including responding to an average of three hundred text messages daily on his well-worn cell phone.

Sometimes, however, the lines between work and leisure become blurred, especially when engaging in the Albanian pastime of *begenisje*, which translates into cultivating relationships with key contacts over a coffee or beer. While acknowledging that the hours are endless and the workload unrelenting, Erion admits that he wouldn't change a thing. "I've got the most exciting job in this town. I'm the happiest kid around."

Launching a Campaign for Social Change

During its first four months, MJAFT! organized 150 activities, including marches, petitions, and protests.

MJAFT! began its work in March 2003 as a four-month, "in your face" media campaign. Every two weeks, the group mobilized public awareness and action around a different issue, including the nation's ailing education system, organized crime, human trafficking, and the archaic practice of blood feuds, in which the relative of someone who has perpetrated a crime can be killed or maimed by the victim's family in retribution.

As a first step, Erion and his co-founders explained their goals to some of the country's leading authors, lawyers, newspaper columnists, and health and education experts, many of whom agreed to serve as informal advisors and continue to do so to this day.

With modest equipment in place and plenty of volunteer support, over the course of those initial four months MJAFT! organized 150 activities, ranging from peaceful marches, petitions, and candlelight vigils to evening graffiti outings and public protests. Many of the events generated substantial media coverage and were accompanied by newspaper editorials penned by prominent MJAFT! allies. Following this initial phase, the group's founders decided to form a nonprofit institution aimed at mobilizing and sustaining citizen action around urgent social issues.

To fund its activities, MJAFT! managed to get most of the goods and services it needed for free. Even today, 60 percent of MJAFT!'s budget takes the form of in-kind contributions, which to date add up to the equivalent of U.S.$1.5 million. Such contributions include legal and accounting assistance, office space, Internet connectivity, meals at local restaurants, transportation, and even gasoline. So successful has MJAFT! been at generating in-kind donations that its staff gets free dental care from a local hygienist.

Over the course of its initial four months MJAFT! organized 150 activities, ranging from peaceful marches, petitions, and candlelight vigils to evening graffiti outings and public protests.

Making Protest Fun

Central to MJAFT!'s approach is making protest fun. During one highly visible campaign stunt, MJAFT! mobilized more than a hundred people to cover the national telecom building with toilet paper to protest rising prices and overall mismanagement of the telecom industry. Eventually, not only did senior executives step down, but prices fell, too.

During another MJAFT!-organized media spectacle, a group of thirty young women volunteered to wear bridal gowns and participate in a mock wedding in front of the prime minister's office. The group was protesting the prime minister's sudden designation of his new wife as "First Lady" of Albania, effectively stripping the title from the president's wife. While nothing changed as a result, photos of the event were carried by several international news services.

MJAFT! volunteers wear wedding gowns as a form of protest.

"We operate like a fire brigade, a rapid-action civic force," explains Erion, whose team relies heavily on cell phones and instant messaging to communicate quickly to its citizen volunteer base. For example, soon after the minister of the interior punched a journalist during a disagreement, MJAFT! sent instant messages to over two hundred reporters, who showed up at the Ministry building promptly thereafter shaking their keys and calling for the official's removal. In just two days, the minister resigned.

In an effort to increase government funding for education, MJAFT! organized students and developed a media campaign demonstrating how poorly Albania's educational attainment rates compared to those of other nations around the world. Following the campaign, the government increased the national education budget by 25 million euros (the equivalent of U.S.$30.4 million), bringing it to 3.1 percent of the country's gross domestic product.

While MJAFT! enjoys growing recognition, its tactics and highly visible targets have earned it some enemies. "If you play with fire you're going to get burned," cautions Erion, relating several occasions when MJAFT! has been the subject of attacks by those implicated in its campaigns. In addition to numerous threats received via email, MJAFT! has undergone more than its share of financial audits. Despite the threats, inconveniences, and false rumors, in Erion's view MJAFT! has become too well known and too influential to be forced out of operation.

"We operate like a fire brigade, a rapid-action civic force," explains Erion, whose team relies heavily on cell phones and instant messaging to communicate quickly to its citizen volunteer base.

MJAFT!'s creative tactics not only mobilize the public, but generate media coverage.

Sustaining a Movement

Erion addresses members of the U.S. Congress.

Says Erion, "Not only will we tell you what you're doing wrong, we'll tell you how to do it right."

Having reached the two-year anniversary of its official launch, MJAFT! now employs over twenty full-time staff at its headquarters in Tirana, with six hundred volunteers offering their assistance at branches in more than a dozen cities. In addition to in-kind donations, MJAFT! has received support from the United Nations; the Organization for Security and Co-operation in Europe (OSCE); the Open Society Institute; the Balkan Trust Fund; the Balkan Children and Youth Foundation; Freedom House; the Rockefeller Brothers Fund; and the governments of Germany, the Netherlands, Norway, Switzerland, the United Kingdom, and the United States.

A vital key to sustaining MJAFT!'s impact has been efforts undertaken by its staff to develop an in-depth understanding of the issues it takes on. A policy branch within its headquarters conducts research and studies issues before making recommendations. Says Erion, "Not only will we tell you what you're doing wrong, we'll tell you how to do it right."

Also important has been measuring public support of MJAFT!'s activities. Toward that end, MJAFT! convinced the Institute of Statistics to conduct a poll among a sample of the population to gauge their support of MJAFT!'s activities. According to the poll, 88 percent of those surveyed thought MJAFT! was doing a great job and should continue its work.

Now that MJAFT!'s reputation has earned international recognition – particularly among youth activists in other countries who have heard of its success and want to learn more – the organization has produced a manual called *Change Is Possible* (available at www.mjaft.org), which explains how to lay the foundation for a successful campaign. In the spring of 2005, MJAFT! also sponsored a weeklong activism festival, "Fast Forward," in which youth from more than twenty countries inside and outside the region came to learn and share ideas for achieving sustained social change.

Still, Erion is clear that MJAFT!'s approach is no franchise model. Such movements need to be born of deep commitment and initiated by individuals who have a real passion and drive to make things change, he says.

MJAFT!'s leadership recognizes that for the system truly to change in Albania, pressure – and incentives – must come from outside, as well as inside, the country. Toward that end, MJAFT! works to raise awareness of its activities and key issues in Albania among important stakeholders beyond the country's borders, including the U.S. Congress and Albanians living abroad. MJAFT!'s efforts are increasingly attracting attention from important places. In endorsing MJAFT!'s work, U.S. Senator Sam Brownback commented, "They [MJAFT!] don't just focus on elections, because they understand that democracy is not just about votes. It's about making civil society work and making government accountable to the people." In 2004, MJAFT! was honored with the United Nations Civil Society Award, presented each year to recognize nongovernmental organizations that "demonstrate a high level of commitment to civil society."

The focus of MJAFT! isn't confined to Albania's borders. For its staff, making Albanians more aware of the plight of others around the world is just as important as getting them to play a more active role in their own country. When news arrived of the devastating tsunami in Asia in late 2004, MJAFT! quickly assembled a volunteer team of medical and logistics personnel to offer support to victims.

At the moment, Erion and his MJAFT! colleagues are satisfied with the organization's ability to spotlight "hot button" issues and mobilize people to take action. Still, they recognize that it is often necessary to work within the system to achieve far-reaching change. Could MJAFT! one day become a political party? For now, Erion rejects the idea in favor of stimulating civic engagement from outside the halls of power.

"Our biggest success has been to restore hope," he says, adding that parents often stop him on the street to offer a hug and say thank you. "To me that's the magic, to bring that spark to people. For completely selfish reasons, people should be involved in activism. It just makes you feel good." ∎

Erion fields questions from reporters following a MJAFT! event.

"MJAFT! (meaning ENOUGH!) is now the most understandable Albanian word at the international level, and a vivid example of the fact that changes are possible."

Antonio Maria Costa
Executive Director United Nations Office on Drugs and Crime
Vienna, Austria

"MJAFT! has inspired civic consciousness by presenting issues in such a way that they are accessible to the majority. Its youthful protagonists are extremely talented and intelligent and that's what makes them so effective."

Edi Rama
Mayor
Tirana, Albania

ADVICE FROM ERION ON:

Preparing for a Campaign

- **Get important people on your side.** MJAFT! relies heavily on its informal network of advisors, including journalists, lawyers, and authors.

- **Excel at getting things for free.** Says Erion, "If people believe in a good cause, they're very willing to give pro bono services."

- **Develop a strategy that maximizes your resources and targets those you want to reach.** "It's important to exert intense pressure, at the right time, in the right place, to the right people," counsels Erion.

- **Make it fun.** MJAFT! events are creative and are conceived as both awareness-raising and social events.

- **Show people the solutions.** Don't focus on the negative.

- **Promote a strong work ethic among staff and volunteers through your example.** "At the end of the day, it's working hard that will be what pays off," says Erion.

Designing and Implementing a Campaign Strategy

- **Start out by identifying your goals and objectives.** What attitudes, behaviors, and policies do you seek to change?

- **Develop your message.** Make it relevant and vivid. Use accurate data to give legitimacy to your message. Don't distort the facts.

- **Identify your audience and get to know them.** Concentrate on a pertinent segment of the population and understand the knowledge and attitudes they bring. MJAFT! conducts interviews, surveys, and focus groups of its target audiences (e.g., students) to gauge their thinking on a given subject.

- **Figure out what tools and materials you need.** Such tools may include newspaper ads, editorials, t-shirts, banners, megaphones, and audio-visual equipment.

- **Choose your strategy.** Identify persons or organizations you know that can help, as well as your media contacts, if you have any.

- **Evaluate outcomes.** Look carefully at what worked and what didn't.

Different Roads to the Same Destination:
A Better World

CHRISTIANE AMANPOUR

CHIEF INTERNATIONAL CORRESPONDENT
CNN

If you are reading this book, chances are you have already found something you feel passionately about, or want to change. Perhaps you're outraged about the plight of street children in your neighborhood, or concerned that your peers are apathetic about the political process. You may have experienced discrimination firsthand and want to help change people's perceptions of those different from themselves. Maybe you are just fed up with all the pollution in the nearby river. The point is, you want to make a difference in the world around you and change it for the better. But how? I was lucky. I knew, quite early, the path I wanted to take.

Kritaya Sreesunpagit champions volunteerism among Thai youth.

From the moment my family and I left Iran after the Islamic revolution, I knew I wanted to be a foreign correspondent. I was 21 at the time, and I felt that if I was going to be affected by events, I wanted to be part of them. I arrived at CNN with a suitcase, my bicycle, and about U.S.$100 – but also with a deep commitment to inform the public and cast a spotlight on stories too often left untold. Effective reporting, I would learn, requires qualities that we all need to succeed – a passion for learning, confidence, perseverance, teamwork, and communications skills. We also need empathy for others and a profound interest in the human condition. Perhaps the most valuable lesson I've learned from more than two decades of journalism is that objectivity must go hand in hand with morality. When you remain neutral in how you portray events, you may be only one step away from being an accomplice to those actions.

I've been struck by the extraordinary drive, determination, and practical wisdom these young leaders have demonstrated, and how much they have been able to accomplish with so little financial or institutional support.

Today, particularly in this increasingly global era, young people can, and must, play a role in shaping the world around them – and that includes using the media to get across their message and their dreams. We desperately need youths' perspectives on some of the most critical issues of our time – education, the environment, human rights, child abuse, the growing divide between rich and poor, and the impact of globalization. While many young people now engaged in some way in reporting or creating the news may never pursue a career in journalism, they will have learned invaluable skills in analyzing events around them, questioning the status quo, and ensuring that the voices of those on the margins of society are heard.

When my son is old enough to ask me what I've done with my life and why I've spent more than twenty years in the field of journalism, I will tell him it's because I'm a believer. I believe that if you tell a compelling story, people will listen. But even more, by revealing today's harsh realities – genocide, starvation, HIV/AIDS – and exposing the bad and successful policies of our politicians, we can have a real impact on what takes place in our local communities, in our countries, and in the world.

In the following pages, you will read about a number of remarkable young people who have found their own unique ways of being agents of change. One of them, Harjant Gill from the United States, has chosen the media to further his goals, using the power of film to highlight gender issues, particularly the ongoing discrimination against gays and lesbians. You will learn about Tang Kun, a medical student in Beijing who organized his fellow students to educate teenagers about how to prevent the spread of HIV/AIDS. Marbie Depayso, who lives in an indigenous community in the northern Philippines, is teaching farmers there how to grow their crops using organic substances. And in the U.K., Mohammed Mamdani has developed a free, confidential, youth-led telephone counseling service that addresses the needs of thousands of young Muslim men and women each year. The list goes on.

I've been struck by the extraordinary drive, determination, and practical wisdom these young leaders have demonstrated, and how much they have been able to accomplish with so little financial or institutional support. Each one of them, in vastly different ways, is helping to create a more democratic, tolerant, open, and hopeful society. I've been deeply inspired by their stories and trust you will be, too. ∎

In the U.S., Harjant Gill uses the power of film to explore issues of identity and belonging.

JAVIER ALEJANDRO LÓPEZ AGUILAR

Implementing a national service-learning initiative

MEXICO

Through his work, Alejandro helps to provide students with the knowledge and skills to contribute to their communities.

Brazilian philosopher and educator Paulo Freire talked about political illiteracy. This is a concept that applies to a large percentage of the Latin American population. It refers to their social exclusion due to lack of access to information and opportunities. It's true. Nobody chooses the conditions in which they were born. However, it's more difficult to change your environment when you come to the world as part of a silenced culture that is never heard. Nowadays, hundreds of thousands of people lack a critical consciousness of how they might influence the economic, political, and social landscape around them. Literacy campaigns, women's rights workshops, and development projects designed by civil society are building this critical conscience.

– Javier Alejandro López Aguilar

OUR TIME IS NOW

Different Roads to the Same Destination: **A Better World**

As a child, Javier Alejandro López Aguilar remembers being carried by his parents to community gatherings near his home on the outskirts of Mexico City. His father, a factory administrator, and mother, a psychologist, knew then that a critical step in improving the plight of the poor was to engage them in finding solutions to community problems. At local citizen forums, his parents would share their ideas for addressing urgent social issues such as women's and workers' rights and public healthcare needs.

A key goal of Parte y Comparte is to broaden the perspectives of students through immersing them in realities different from their own.

The origins of Alejandro's own commitment to social justice can be traced back to those early years. As an eighth-grade student, Alejandro became involved in a literacy project, teaching poor people in rural communities how to read and write. While according to official statistics, 17 percent of Mexico's population is illiterate, that figure rises as high as 75 percent in some rural communities, according to Alejandro. Educating citizens and mobilizing them to play an active role in shaping their own reality would become a major theme in Alejandro's work.

Now 20, Alejandro serves as a trainer for and advisor to the "Parte y Comparte" (Give and Share) program, which works to nurture a spirit of volunteerism among Mexican high school and college students. Parte y Comparte is a national service-learning initiative of Servicios a la Juventud AC (SERAJ), a nongovernmental organization. Service learning is a process whereby students acquire practical knowledge through contributing to their communities – knowledge that is reinforced through customized curricula and instruction.

By providing young people with opportunities to get engaged in their communities, Alejandro seeks to plant seeds of civic participation that will last a lifetime. As part of its mission, Parte y Comparte equips youth with valuable skills, such as how to manage a project and deliver a service. An added goal is transforming the public perception that young people are problems to be solved. Instead, the program demonstrates young people's active role in implementing solutions.

Over the past three years, Parte y Comparte has worked in more than a hundred schools, reaching over two thousand young people in seven states in Mexico. The efforts of these young people have, in turn, impacted the lives of more than forty-two thousand children, youth, and families. In some communities, parents are now better equipped to meet the health and nutritional needs of their children, while in others, young people have a greater understanding of reproductive health issues and steps they can take to prevent the spread of HIV/AIDS. In still others, once illiterate adults are learning how to read and write, and young women have gained a better understanding of their rights.

Equipping Students with Practical Skills

Alejandro's commitment to Parte y Comparte is rooted in its ability to build bridges of understanding between students and people of all ages who are living in poor, marginalized communities. Many participants choose volunteer activities that take them to often-forgotten parts of the country, where they live with host families or in makeshift group homes provided by local authorities.

Those who know Alejandro well view his youth and enthusiasm for "giving back" as valuable assets.

"The lives of those living in poor, rural communities are no longer a mystery hidden away from these youth, but a reality," says Alejandro, adding that students come to realize that these people are a vital part of the "national identity." "Being poor is not a problem," he emphasizes, "but a consequence of inhuman politics and an imbalanced system."

Every week, Alejandro devotes an average of thirty-five hours to various social development projects, while juggling the responsibilities of completing a university degree in economics. Among his work-related duties, Alejandro has played a lead role in designing Parte y Comparte's curriculum, training local trainers to work in schools, and overseeing the implementation of the program in different parts of the country.

While his age has sometimes posed a barrier – for example, in approaching foundations and government agencies to support his ideas – those who know Alejandro well view his youth and enthusiasm for "giving back" as valuable assets. "Alejandro has been a key person in bringing the project to life," says Gustavo Hernández, national coordinator of Parte y Comparte. "Alejandro is an innovator who always comes up with new ideas to improve the project," he adds, "and has a wonderful way of communicating with people of all ages."

Parte y Comparte is carried out in several stages, beginning with teaching students about the value of service and the importance of developing empathy for others' lives, needs, and concerns. During the second stage of the program, students learn basic life skills, such as how to plan a project, manage their time, communicate effectively, work as a team, and resolve conflicts. Next, the students visit

Community members have the opportunity to express themselves through art.

A Parte y Comparte launch event in Zongolica.

the community they plan to serve and interview local residents about their needs. Afterward, the volunteers develop a work plan and receive training in how to deliver services. Training modules focus on different topics, such as teaching reading and writing skills, gender equality, children's rights, and health and nutrition. Finally, the students spend three to four weeks in the summer living and working in the community, carrying out their project and analyzing the results.

Participants who successfully complete the first year of the program are then invited back to serve as mentors and advisors to subsequent volunteer groups. Alumni who express a strong interest in the program may also qualify as trainers.

Applying Knowledge Gained in the Classroom

For some Parte y Comparte participants, the experience of immersing themselves in a completely different reality proves life changing. Over the past three years, for example, high school students from Mexico City have applied what they learned in the classroom to addressing the needs of young people and women in five low-income communities surrounding the town of Zongolica in the state of Veracruz.

Alejandro tells the story of one group of twenty volunteers that arrived in Zongolica in 2004. During the day, the students broke into groups, traveling by city bus to their respective locations. One group, for example, spent time mentoring local children in how to express themselves through art. Every morning, the volunteers were greeted by a dozen or so eager pupils in a small wooden house, where the children would receive instruction and encouragement in how to draw, make masks, and construct piñatas. For these children, the experience offered a rare chance to explore their creativity, while also interacting with positive role models.

Another team met with young mothers who could neither read nor write. Slowly, the participating mothers gained confidence in their abilities, with many accessing local literacy programs after the volunteers' departure. For such women, learning to read and write can be enormously empowering, says Alejandro. Simple tasks, like learning how to sign one's name, can open a door to opportunities they might not otherwise be able to access.

Still another group traveled to a nearby neighborhood where they met with teenagers to talk about health issues and HIV/AIDS prevention – subjects the local teens were far more receptive to learning about from trained peers than from teachers. For these local youth, as is the case for young people in other communities where Parte y

Participants in a student-led writing course receive their diplomas.

Comparte operates, the interest of the volunteers in their communities translates into a greater sense of pride and empowerment for leading positive changes themselves. Says Alejandro, "The workshops provide adolescents with information and motivation. They come to view themselves the way SERAJ views them – as actors in society and as transformers."

Over time, the volunteers, too, expand their view of the world and their place in it. When they first arrived in Zongolica, notes Alejandro, the volunteers didn't interact much, preferring to associate with those they knew well. Such barriers quickly dissolved as the group started living together and pursuing shared goals. Initially, the volunteers were also apprehensive about their temporary home – a modest building that was otherwise used to house the relatives of patients at a local hospital. Alejandro remembers that the volunteers started the month "thinking about how ugly the place they slept was." Slowly attitudes began to shift as the volunteers immersed themselves in local realities. By the last week of their stay, the students took action to clean, repair, and paint their temporary home. "They loved it," says Alejandro, "and were eager to return the next year."

Alejandro also notes changes in the volunteers' values and aspirations. "A significant portion of them are greatly influenced by their summer experience," he notes. "Many start rethinking their career goals. They interact differently with their families at home and change their perceptions about their country and their roles in society."

Partly as a result of his work with Parte y Comparte, Alejandro himself is rethinking how he would like to maximize his contributions to society. In the future, he hopes to collaborate with a group of friends in launching an NGO that would mobilize resources to strengthen community development initiatives. ■

Alejandro works with students from the Vista Hermosa school to evaluate their project.

"As someone committed to social progress and change from a very young age, I consider youth leadership as vital to transforming our world. Young people's voices need to be heard, and our commitment to today's youth must transcend borders, races, and cultures. To the young people reading this book, I can only say, 'Go for it! Take action for what you believe in.' The world needs your integrity, your energy, and your optimism."

Ricky Martin
President Ricky Martin Foundation
San Juan, Puerto Rico

ADVICE FROM ALEJANDRO ON:

Launching Service-Learning Activities

- **Demonstrate your enthusiasm; teach through your example.** "People get excited when they see others who have conviction and who enjoy the work they do," says Alejandro. "Look for ways of communicating the joy of learning and the discovery process that awaits students as they explore local realities."

- **Be careful to create modules that are flexible and that empower participating students to make decisions.** Students involved in Parte y Comparte's work are free to develop their own responses to needs that they themselves identify in the community.

- **Share decision-making.** Teamwork is essential to carrying out effective service-learning activities, emphasizes Alejandro. "Try not to decide things alone," he cautions. "Always consult with participating students."

- **Strive for local ownership of the program.** While Parte y Comparte is a national service-learning initiative, Alejandro notes that its long-term success depends on local schools adopting its approach and engaging parents, teachers, and community members in supporting its objectives. "Such steps are important if the project is to eventually be owned by schools and students," he says.

- **Strive to avoid public perceptions of service activities as "charity."** It's important to reinforce among community members who are receiving assistance that student-led service activities are not charitable acts, but rather are aimed at empowering local citizens to play an active role in addressing their own needs.

- **Be patient; gaining trust takes time.** Alejandro stresses the importance of building relationships with local communities over time. Student-led efforts are likely to be far better received if people know they will be continued, he says. Also, take care to collaborate with local NGOs in identifying community needs and ensuring that those services developed are appropriate.

- **Monitor your results.** Engage students in monitoring the project's impact, advises Alejandro, and "promise only what you can deliver."

MARBIE DEPAYSO

Promoting sustainable, organic agriculture

THE PHILIPPINES

After reading newspaper reports about the growing use of genetically modified organisms and chemicals in the Cordilleras, I became more and more convinced of the need to go into organic agriculture. I realized that I had to do something good for my community, especially because most of my community members are farmers, who work so hard every day. I knew that if they continued their existing farming practices, they could end up losers. Their land would not be as fertile, and most of their capital would end up in the hands of chemical companies.

– Marbie Depayso

Through promoting organic agriculture, Marbie advocates for a return to the ways of the past.

Farming is a way of life for many indigenous groups in the Philippines.

The rugged Caraballo Mountains of the northern Philippines are home to a number of indigenous tribes – Bugkalot, Kalanguya, Ibaloi, Kankana-ey, Ifugao, Kalinga, and Bontoc. For centuries, such indigenous peoples have lived in a delicate balance with nature, sustaining themselves and their families off the land. Yet today, many find themselves struggling to preserve a traditional way of life and culture while navigating the forces of change around them.

Change and so-called "development" often come with a price, as 23-year-old Marbie Depayso came to learn. A member of the Kankana-ey tribe, Marbie has spent most of her life in the village of Dupax, a sprawling community with roughly fifty homes scattered atop the surrounding hills. The eldest of six children, Marbie has long played a key role in managing her family's modest farm. In 2004, Marbie participated in a leadership training course through Make a Connection, a global life skills education program of the International Youth Foundation and Nokia. As a result of the course, she became increasingly concerned about the level of pesticides and fertilizers being used by local farmers – a trend that has grown throughout the Philippines, as in other countries.

"While farmers have more options, they are often not taught the proper use of these substances," says Marbie, pointing to documented cases in which the land and groundwater surrounding farms in the northern Philippines have grown contaminated, or cases in which farmers have misused chemicals and suffered ill health as a result. According to Marbie, the potential health risks of heavy pesticide and fertilizer use can include kidney trouble, skin diseases, respiratory infections, and even cancer. Especially vulnerable are children, she adds, who are more susceptible to chemicals and can develop respiratory problems as a result of direct exposure.

"While farmers have more options, they are often not taught the proper use of these substances," says Marbie.

Recognizing the growth of the agrochemical industry in the Philippines, Marbie is particularly concerned about the role of large companies in marketing products to small-scale farmers that they might not necessarily need, and that may, in the long run, adversely impact the land's productivity. Currently, more than 1,300 fertilizer and pesticide products are sold in the

Philippines, according to Marbie, with nearly 300 additional products approved for experimental use. Farmers frequently don't exercise the right precautions when applying such chemicals, she points out. Furthermore, heavy reliance upon chemical fertilizers and pesticides can threaten soil fertility, notes Marbie, through killing valuable microorganisms that help sustain the soil.

Learning and Then Teaching Others

As participants in the leadership training course, Marbie and a number of her peers brainstormed ideas for boosting the productivity of local farms through natural, as opposed to artificial, means. Following the training, they registered their own nongovernmental organization, the Genuine Association of Indigenous Youth Tribes of Dupax, Inc. (GAIYTDI). GAIYTDI's mission: to raise the standard of living among the region's indigenous peoples through sustainable farming practices.

Currently, GAIYTDI comprises more than fifty youth members, who carry out public education and advocacy work in six *barangays*, or village districts, in the surrounding area. Part of what makes GAIYTDI unique is that it brings together local youth representing three tribal groups – the Bugkalot, Kalanguya, and Kankana-ey – that have often been in conflict with one another. Through working together toward a shared goal of environmental sustainability, GAIYTDI's members are modeling a new way of living and interacting for the surrounding community.

Working from a small office equipped with a typewriter, a few tables, and some chairs, GAIYTDI staff co-ordinates various outreach activities, including demonstrations on how to make organic fertilizer, field trips to local farms that have successfully integrated organic practices, and hands-on trainings. The group has constructed a mill to process organic rice and is planting tree seedlings on hillsides that were deforested by irresponsible logging practices. Recent flash floods and landslides in nearby provinces have reinforced among GAIYTDI's members the importance of preserving their natural surroundings.

As GAIYTDI's accountant, Marbie maintains the financial records for its various projects, which include a loan fund and the buying and processing of unmilled rice for local consumption. Much of her work is conducted at her family's kitchen table. Using a cell phone, Marbie mobilizes GAIYTDI members and volunteers to conduct trainings and carry out advocacy efforts.

GAIYTDI established its revolving loan fund with financial resources provided by the Consuelo Foundation, a national nonprofit serving children and youth; Nokia; and Tribal Cooperation for Rural Development, Inc. (TRICORD, a local nongovernmental

Marbie's commitment to organic farming grew as a result of a leadership training course she attended.

Currently, GAIYTDI comprises more than fifty youth members, who carry out public education and advocacy work in six barangays, or village districts.

organization). Through the fund, farmers may apply for micro-loans to help them integrate organic farming methods into their production.

Organic farming can be achieved through the use of readily available local substances, such as leaves and fermented plant juice, says Marbie.

Loans of up to U.S.$180 are payable within six months, with an interest rate of 6 percent per year, plus a 5 percent annual fee. To date, twenty GAIYTDI members have received loans.

Marbie herself took out a loan of five thousand Philippine pesos (the equivalent of U.S.$90) to grow *yacon*, a potato-like root vegetable, on her family's farm using organic fertilizer and pesticides. Organic farming can be achieved through the use of readily available local substances, emphasizes Marbie, including fermented plant juice; leaves from local plants and trees; and vermi-composting, which uses red worms to quickly convert organic kitchen and garden waste into fertilizer.

Says Marbie, "While people are generally receptive, and some have already introduced organic farming to their respective farms, the impact [of our efforts] is not yet totally felt."

Leading with Integrity

With her slight build and gentle demeanor, Marbie continues to surprise many local villagers with her passion for leading change in the community. She acknowledges that one of the biggest challenges she faces is being a woman in a largely male-dominated society. She attributes her success in transforming people's behaviors to her personal integrity and accomplishments, including the undergraduate degree in secondary education she earned at a state-run college.

GAIYTDI members blend organic fertilizer.

Elsa Ravelo, senior program specialist at the Consuelo Foundation, which cosponsored the leadership training Marbie and the others received, speaks enthusiastically of Marbie's recent contributions. "In the very patriarchal society of the indigenous people, Marbie stands out," she says. "The fact that she is very low key and unassuming makes her more successful at being a role model for other young girls and women in her community. She has become very influential, even among the men, because she does not threaten them or upset cultural norms."

Marbie admits that had she not become so involved in promoting organic agriculture in the region, she might have left her village to pursue opportunities elsewhere. She largely credits the leadership training course she participated in with helping her develop the knowledge and confidence she needed to foster positive change in her community.

She also takes comfort in knowing that the organic farming practices she advocates are similar to those her people employed for generations. Marbie sees her current role as "planting a seed in the farmers' hearts," explaining, "We are optimistic that little by little it will grow into full bloom." ■

Marbie serves as GAIYTDI's accountant. The group's office is a simple space where records are kept and organic agricultural practices are demonstrated.

"Whether preserving the environment or educating children about their rights, today's young social entrepreneurs offer innovative solutions to a host of urgent global challenges. Working with scant resources and a wealth of determination, they demonstrate that positive change is not only possible, but is happening every day in communities around the world."

Jaime Augusto Zobel de Ayala II
President and CEO Ayala Corporation
Makati City, Philippines

ADVICE FROM MARBIE ON:

Leading Environmental Change

- **Develop expertise in your issue.** Marbie and her peers spent months conducting feasibility studies and learning about organic agricultural practices so they could back up their advocacy efforts with solid evidence. Likewise, they underwent training and sought outside expertise in establishing their organizational and financial structure.

- **Develop a team.** Marbie joined with a number of other area youth in identifying local challenges and proposing solutions. Together, they planned and implemented joint activities aimed at promoting sustainable, organic agriculture in their communities.

- **When advocating a change in people's behavior, attitudes, and values, set an example through your own actions.** In promoting organic agricultural practices, GAIYTDI sets up pilot projects where people can see how organic fertilizers and pesticides are made and used. At trainings and public presentations, GAIYTDI staff and volunteers relate their own personal experiences in implementing organic practices.

- **Emphasize simple solutions.** Marbie and other GAIYTDI members champion the use of readily available plants and natural waste to replace chemical fertilizers and pesticides. In advocating their cause to local farmers, they emphasize a return to the ways of the past. "Our ancestors sustained their lives without so many complications using traditional practices," notes Marbie. "Let us live in harmony with nature. Let us go organic!"

- **Don't give up.** While admitting that it's been difficult and time consuming to convince people to change their behaviors, Marbie emphasizes that you can't let such difficulties stop you. There's a good chance that your efforts are part of a larger movement underway in other places. Says Marbie, "I believe others can learn from us as we can learn from them."

HARJANT GILL

Using the power of film to spotlight gender issues

UNITED STATES

A scene from Mission Movie, *a feature film Harjant coproduced.*

All of my films address issues of identity and belonging. These are general themes and struggles all of us can relate to and have experienced. So when I screen my films and people tell me that they were able to connect with a character, or were able to relate to him or her, or saw themselves reflected in that person, that to me is most critical. It's then that I know I've been successful as a filmmaker. It's that connection that you spend countless hours trying to achieve. As a filmmaker, that's what you live for. That's what you make films for.

– Harjant Gill

For Harjant Gill, making films is about casting a spotlight on urgent, and often overlooked, social issues. It's also about making marginalized members of society – gays, lesbians, and other minority groups – feel less isolated and more understood. As a 23-year-old social activist who also happens to be gay and an Indian immigrant to the United States, Harjant knows what it can feel like to be socially excluded and alone.

Says Harjant, "I make documentary films that help raise the self-esteem of the gay community because we're so bombarded with messages that we're a minority and being gay is wrong. Eventually it takes a toll on your self-esteem."

Over the past five years, Harjant has directed or produced four films and a number of videos that highlight complex gender and race issues. A recent graduate of San Francisco State University, where he completed a degree in cultural anthropology and filmmaking, Harjant believes strongly in the power of art, and film in particular, to serve as a social change agent. "My work has and always will tell stories of oppression," he says, adding that his films are dedicated to "getting others to see outside their box and within a larger societal context."

In *Some Reasons for Living*, *Harjant explores the lives of two transgender Latina women.*

Making Films: A Powerful Means of Self-Expression and Public Education

Born in India to traditional Sikh parents, Harjant moved with his family to the United States at the age of 15. A year later, he announced that he was gay. The reaction at school was all too common. "My locker was broken into; people would make derogatory comments," he recalls. The process of telling his parents was made even more difficult given that in India, the issue of homosexuality is so repressed that there is hardly any terminology in place to define it. While his parents were initially disturbed and attempted to change his mind, they've now come to accept his sexual orientation.

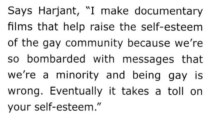

"My work has and always will tell stories of oppression," says Harjant, adding that his films are dedicated to "getting others to see outside their box and within a larger societal context."

Harjant's first exposure to filmmaking came a few years later when, at the age of 19, he became involved in a video project through the Gay-Straight Alliance Network and TILT, a media-literacy training program that teaches students to understand and create their own media messages. The twenty-five-minute film, *As If It Matters...*, tells the stories of six high school students and explores issues related to homophobia, cultural acceptance, body image, relationships, and stereotypes. Since the film was produced, it's been distributed through Gay-Straight Alliances at more than four hundred middle and high schools throughout California and other parts of the United States, along with an accompanying curriculum aimed at combating prejudice against gay and lesbian youth.

"Every film festival it's gone to, people come up to me and say, 'I've experienced the same thing,'" comments Harjant.

Says Harjant, "It [the film] opened a creative door through which I found my Wonderland. I thought, 'Wow, this is a powerful medium.'" Still, he admits it's always been the Issues that drive his work. Even in his early teen years, Harjant recalls being a "social issues junkie," who closely followed the art cinema scene in India, with its focus on women's rights, the caste system, and other topics related to social injustice.

At 20, Harjant conceived of his solo directorial debut, *EVERYTHING*, engaging several friends and even recruiting his twin brother as the lead actor.

He managed to produce the eight-minute film for less than U.S.$200, borrowing a friend's camera and editing the piece on a library computer. Says Harjant, "I wanted to make a film about something important. I wanted to tell the story of being Indian and coming out in high school. . . . When you're passionate about an issue, you don't care as much about where you're going to get the funding. You just do it."

Through this fictionalized autobiography, Harjant tells of his own struggle to be accepted and to belong. Viewers are exposed to the myriad challenges a young gay Indian male faces both at home and at school, including homophobia, alienation, and even suicidal thoughts. Over the past three years, *EVERYTHING* has been showcased at film festivals around the U.S., as well as in Canada and India.

Harjant refers to *EVERYTHING* as the most satisfying film he's made. Although at first he was fearful that people outside the Indian culture wouldn't be able to relate to the film, those doubts quickly evaporated. "Every film festival it's gone to, people come up to me and say, 'I've experienced the same thing,'" he comments. Deeply gratified by the film's cross-cultural appeal, Harjant explains that even people in their 40s and 50s who are not Indian attest that they can relate to its content.

Societal alienation and community building are potent themes in Harjant's work.

Different Roads to the Same Destination: **A Better World**

Harjant's subsequent film, *Some Reasons for Living*, examines the day-to-day struggles of two transgender Latina women, their sisterly relationship, and their reflections on love and life in general. Viewers also learn of the discrimination they face and the grim fact that because of their gender identity, they are more likely to become victims of a hate crime than members of any other minority group.

Says Harjant, "The project made me realize how much gender is taken for granted in our society and how easily we can alienate and outcast those who do not fit into our rigidly defined, black-and-white ideologies around sexuality and gender."

With each successive project, Harjant has enhanced his knowledge of not only film production, but also the nuances of marketing and distribution. Still, he admits there are many technical aspects of filmmaking, such as lighting and audio recording, that he defers to others. His real interests and gifts lie in conceptualizing storylines, directing, and producing.

His most recent project, *Mission Movie*, is a feature film exploring the diversity of life and relationships in San Francisco's Mission District. Based on a true story, the film's multiethnic tapestry includes the

Harjant enjoys a playful moment with the cast and crew of Mission Movie.

experiences of a newly arrived Mexican family and the conflict of values experienced within a Palestinian family. The film has received critical acclaim at a number of film festivals across the U.S. and is in distribution.

Harjant's most recent project, Mission Movie, *is a feature film exploring the diversity of life and relationships in San Francisco's Mission District.*

Harjant notes that what made *Mission Movie* unique was the engagement of the entire community in its production. "A community of people made the film, not just a bunch of actors and directors," he says, adding that the sharing of ideas creates not only a better product, but also a more satisfying experience overall.

Bridging social divides and nurturing a sense of shared community are potent themes in Harjant's work. "In order for us to get along and share a space, we need to understand each other's differences," he emphasizes. "You can live in isolation or you can live in an engaged way. By being more engaged, you realize the value of neighborhood, of community, and [of] society."

Looking Ahead

As his next project, Harjant is collaborating on a screenplay that will explore the theme of gay marriage. Having recently been accepted into American University's Ph.D. Program in Anthropology, he plans to devote this new chapter of his academic career to exploring issues related to human rights, homosexuality, and the AIDS pandemic in India.

Asked about his artistic role models in life, Harjant quickly references Indian actress and social activist Shabana Azmi, whom he paraphrases as having said: "I don't think films can bring about great transformation in individual people's lives. But I think all art has the ability to create a climate of sensitivity in which it is possible for social change to occur." Harjant acknowledges that he became a filmmaker for the very same purpose. He also finds inspiration in the artistry of film directors Pedro Almodóvar and Deepa Mehta, as well as novelist James Baldwin and jazz singer Nina Simone.

As for his family, Harjant says his parents have come to accept the fact that he is gay, and they no longer fear that he will end up homeless and penniless as a result of his life choices. Their only real criticism these days, he notes, is the way he wears his hair in dreadlocks – a form of self-expression he's in no hurry to change. ∎

Mission Movie *explores the diversity of life and relationships in San Francisco's Mission District.*

"In a world where, increasingly, art is bowing to commercial considerations, it is heartening to find young filmmakers like Harjant Gill who have the courage to use their art as an instrument for social change."

Shabana Azmi
Actress
Goodwill Ambassador United Nations Population Fund
Mumbai, India

"When I started making documentary films, I had to tap my engineering training to devise equipment that allowed me to record sound and pictures the way I wanted. Even then it was cumbersome and demanded a certain amount of training, which I got by working with and observing others. All that has changed – is changing as you read this in a most amazing way. The cost or bulk of equipment is no longer a real constraint for filmmaking. The world is filling now with Harjant Gills, who will tell personal stories and open up new worlds for the rest of us."

D A Pennebaker
Award-Winning Documentary Filmmaker
The War Room, Monterey Pop, Don't Look Back
New York, New York, United States

ADVICE FROM HARJANT ON:

Making Your First Film or Video

- **If you want to learn about filmmaking, watch films.** At a young age, Harjant became interested in the type of films and subjects he now pursues in his own work. He urges budding filmmakers to watch films with a critical eye, to identify the issues a particular filmmaker is trying to address, and to explore each film's possible impact on the larger society.

- **Choose an issue or subject you feel passionate about.** The more passion and excitement you have for a given subject, the more you will be able to convince others to support your efforts, says Harjant. Having a great story – a story you believe in – can make up for a lack of technical expertise.

- **Don't be afraid to start small.** The first film Harjant directed, *EVERYTHING*, lasts only eight minutes. Longer isn't necessarily better, says Harjant, who is often most inspired by shorter films.

- **Put together a team of people who possess the skills and experience you need.** For those starting out, finding technical experts to help with editing and producing a project can alleviate the pressure of having to master a lot of technical details right away. Says Harjant, "Just as it takes a village to raise a child, it takes a lot more than one person to make a successful feature or documentary."

- **Don't let a lack of funding stop you from realizing your dream.** Harjant made his first video for less than U.S.$200 using a borrowed camera and software he was able to access on a library computer. He has also succeeded in obtaining small grants for his work.

- **Try to engage organizations that share a commitment to your issue.** Such organizations can be helpful as you shape the content of your film or video. They may also provide seed funding, host a private screening, or assist with distribution of your work.

- **Consider submitting your finished work to film festivals and competitions.** Much of the acclaim Harjant's work has received came initially from film festival audiences.

TANG KUN

Engaging college students in the fight against HIV/AIDS

CHINA

The first time I met a person with HIV, I was deeply moved by her courage and spirit. She was a writer, the same age as me. She gave me a book written by her as a present. It was a book about the life and situation of HIV carriers in China, a rather sad story, based on a year she spent talking with carriers in different cities of China to gather their firsthand data. Probably it was the first book ever in China that was written by an HIV carrier about the true life of those infected with the disease. At the end of our conversation, she asked me whether she could sign her name on the first page. I could feel strongly that she wanted to be a successful writer and, like other famous writers, sign her name on her work for readers in bookstores. But now she couldn't because of the stigma and discrimination that existed in people's minds about the disease.

– Tang Kun

The Peer Education Programme bases its approach on the notion that young people are often best equipped to communicate reproductive health messages to their peers.

OUR TIME IS NOW
PAGE 97

SECTION TWO
Different Roads to the Same Destination: **A Better World**

At 19, Tang Kun was just beginning his medical studies at Peking University when he met an HIV-infected author, not much older than himself. Moved by the young woman's story and the apparent shame she felt, Tang took action to help prevent not only the disease's spread, but also the social isolation experienced by those with HIV/AIDS. Recalls Tang, "I wanted more people, especially the young, to realize that those with AIDS are part of our society and have the same rights as we have. Stigma and discrimination won't help cure the disease."

Current official estimates place the number of HIV/AIDS-infected people in China at nearly a million, more than 60 percent of whom are under the age of 24. According to the United Nations Programme on HIV/AIDS, the number of Chinese citizens with the disease could go as high as ten million by 2010 if the epidemic is left unchecked. Tang realized that educating the nation's youth would be critical to combating the disease. "It became clear to me that the reason we can't effectively prevent AIDS from spreading is that most Chinese people lack basic knowledge on AIDS – especially youth," emphasizes Tang.

As a young person and an aspiring health professional, Tang also knew that youth often listen to and learn best about reproductive health messages when such messages come from those their own age. "Peer education," he says, "emerged as an effective way to solve the problem, as it is warmly welcomed by students."

With a basic strategy in mind – and with growing support among his fellow students and professors – Tang launched the Peer Education Programme in 2002. In doing so, he capitalized on his position as president of Peking University's School of Basic Medical Sciences Student Union, tapping university resources and eventually embedding the initiative within the institution's formal structure.

Over a short period of time, Tang convinced prominent nongovernmental organizations – the International Federation of Red Cross and Red Crescent Societies, Marie Stopes International–China (MSI-China), and the China Family Planning Association – to provide technical support to the student-led effort. The program received an added boost in early 2004 when Tang was awarded an individual grant from the Ford Foundation in China and the group received additional financial support from MSI-China. A year and a half later, the program had successfully trained over fifty youth as peer educators, whose efforts had reached more than 2,200 high school and university students.

By mid-2005, the Peer Education Programme had reached more than 2,200 high school and university students.

OUR TIME IS NOW

Making the Case to Schools

So how did a medical student accustomed to spending endless hours studying or in class find time to launch a volunteer project? It wasn't easy, says Tang, who took to heart the Hippocratic oath he pledged upon entering medical school: in short, that he would always be ready to help others within his knowledge and ability. Personal exposure to the HIV/AIDS crisis motivated Tang to apply his knowledge in practical ways. "Most students evaluate success by their marks," he explains. "I think it's just as important to really do something."

Tang faced a number of obstacles in turning his idea into a reality. First, he needed to mobilize his fellow students to take precious time away from their medical studies to receive training, assist with program coordination, and facilitate school talks. Medical school students feel enormous pressure to get superior grades and succeed, explains Tang: "Chinese students are very practical and need to know if they'll benefit from their volunteer work." By setting an example himself, and engaging well-known international organizations, Tang succeeded in enticing students to get involved.

Second was the challenge of persuading school administrators of the group's qualifications and the need for HIV/AIDS peer education in schools. "School authorities were hard to convince," comments Tang, noting that many had given up on efforts to teach reproductive health to students

given the sensitivity of communicating issues related to sexuality. Tang's own experiences as a high school student confirmed this reality. "When we got to the chapter in our biology textbooks on human reproduction, the teacher asked us to read it ourselves," he recalls. In advocating the need for peer-led reproductive health education in schools, Tang took time to strengthen his own knowledge base around the disease and again reinforced the role that other organizations were willing to play.

And finally, there was Tang's propensity toward shyness. "I'm not so outgoing," confesses Tang, who admits his natural tendency would be to read books in his spare time. Tang worked on developing his communication skills, recognizing that he would need to assert himself to achieve the project's goals.

Serving as president of the Student Union not only helped Tang hone his presentation skills, but also gave him a visible platform for launching the program. Asked whether he sees himself as a leader, Tang says he prefers to be viewed as a server. "I think a leader is someone who sends out commands, but I don't," he says. "I'm just making a connection between those who want to help and those who need help."

University students receive peer education training in Beijing.

"When we got to the chapter in our biology textbooks on human reproduction, the teacher asked us to read it ourselves," recalls Tang.

Launching a Peer Education Initiative

Tang distributes informational materials during a school visit.

Tang started out by garnering letters of support from senior faculty within the university and networking with health-related organizations such as MSI-China, which provided technical support and educational leaflets and posters. An initial cadre of medical school student volunteers received training in HIV/AIDS-prevention education from Marie Stopes, while the Red Cross provided supplementary training on gender equality and volunteerism. Tang also tapped a number of services available through the Student Union. For example, the foreign contact department was charged with approaching schools and organizing trainings; the publication department designed posters and leaflets; and the finance department maintained the group's accounting records.

The program began with two key audiences in mind: university and high school students. Tang accessed the first group through carefully lobbying university administrators. "In China, if you want to do something you must establish good relationships with those around you, especially those in charge," he says.

With a core group of trainers fully prepared, in 2002 Tang and his fellow medical students organized events at five universities, including the China Agricultural University, the Beijing Foreign Language Institute, and the University of Posts and Telecommunications, where more than five hundred students showed up. Famous AIDS activists were also recruited to serve as guest lecturers for the event.

In early 2004, Tang began work on the Ford Foundation–funded project, which targeted area high schools and students at Peking University. The training techniques used – presentations followed by small-group discussions – represented a dramatic departure from traditional teaching methods in China. "This kind of education is quite new to Chinese students, who usually recite and record what the teacher says," explains Tang. "Students liked the interactivity."

What took place during a typical classroom session? To begin, students filled out a brief questionnaire to gauge their level of knowledge about HIV/AIDS. Afterward they participated in warm-up exercises, such as relating their favorite hobby or repeating a series of movements led by the peer educator. Games were then introduced to improve students' understanding of how the disease is transmitted and how it works within the body to attack the immune system. In one such game, students gathered in a circle and held hands, with one individual asked to stand inside, while two to three stood on the outside and tried to break through the ring of bodies symbolizing the immune system. In another exercise, students explored true and false beliefs about pathways of transmission; identifying, for example, whether the disease can be transmitted through a mosquito bite, through using public washrooms, or by shaking hands. Interspersed throughout the activities were presentations on high-risk behaviors and prevention strategies.

As a result of such classroom exercises, more than two thousand high school and university students have become better educated about the HIV/AIDS crisis and how to prevent the disease. Peer education is now also offered as an elective course at Peking University.

Looking to the Future

In early 2005, Tang was offered – and accepted – an internship with the United Nations Population Fund (UNFPA) in New York. His university colleagues have continued the Peer Education Programme in his absence, with Tang contributing to their efforts, especially in planning for the program's sustainability. In the future, he envisions the program will train many more volunteers and reach a greater number of students. He'd also like to expand the program to rural areas with high HIV/AIDS infection rates – not only providing prevention education, but also assisting HIV/AIDS patients and children orphaned by the disease.

More and more, Tang views himself as "a seed that passes on knowledge of adolescent health care and AIDS prevention until one day understanding of reproductive health and a positive attitude toward those with HIV/AIDS will be prevalent in our society. Only then," he says, "will we find that every little bit of peer education has educated the ignorant, dismissed prejudice, and promoted the development of our society." ■

"The peer educators invite students to actively participate in discussions and classroom activities, a relatively new phenomenon in China," says Tang.

"Our Time Is Now focuses on young change-makers who aren't afraid to take a stand on important issues. Although facing the demands of medical school, Tang Kun chose to rally his peers around an important cause. As a result of his efforts, thousands of high school and university students in China have a better understanding of how to prevent the spread of HIV/AIDS, and have a greater sensitivity to those with the disease. The GlobalTribe Network celebrates and supports the contributions of young people like Tang Kun, who have courageously illuminated a path for others to follow."

Amy Eldon
Executive Director GlobalTribe Network (USA)
Los Angeles, California, United States

ADVICE FROM TANG ON:

Launching a Peer Education Initiative in Schools

- **Fine-tune your communication skills and build the case for your program.** School administrators can be tough to convince, says Tang, and will want to see evidence that your program is thoroughly researched and works.

- **Be sensitive to the needs of volunteers.** In China, Tang points out, volunteers like to receive recognition for their efforts. To meet this expectation, those peer educators in his program who successfully complete three school presentations receive a special certificate. He is also careful to invest time in building positive relationships with volunteers through hosting parties in his home, for example.

- **Form partnerships with established organizations.** To gain credibility for his project, Tang networked with prominent non-governmental organizations (NGOs) such as the International Federation of Red Cross and Red Crescent Societies, Marie Stopes International–China, and the China Family Planning Association, all of which provided him with technical support and lent legitimacy to the group's efforts.

- **Invest in high-quality training.** Peer educators need to know not only the substance of what they are teaching, but also how to creatively engage students in learning the material. It's important to access trainers who are experienced in your issue and in working with the audience you are targeting.

- **Make the information accessible to students.** Convey your message using language and tools that students will gravitate toward. Tang's group uses interactive games to help engage students and ensure that they truly understand the material.

- **Set up systems for monitoring and evaluating results.** Tang emphasizes the importance of collecting baseline data regarding your target group's level of knowledge about your issue before you begin classroom instruction. Toward this end, his initiative administers a questionnaire at the beginning of each class. Similarly, it's important to measure the extent to which students retain the knowledge provided.

MOHAMMED MAMDANI

Providing telephone support services for Muslim youth

UNITED KINGDOM

As a young Muslim growing up in the U.K., I was all too familiar with the problems young Muslims face. The alienation and isolation of Muslim youth was not something I noticed; it was something I lived with, along with my peers. It was something we endured, something we knew was worth changing. In college, I became more and more aware of the emotional anguish experienced by my friends, many of whom suffered mental health problems or used drugs as a means of escaping their anxieties, fears, and problems.

– Mohammed Mamdani

Since 2001, the Muslim Youth Helpline, a free, confidential telephone counseling service in the U.K., has responded to more than ten thousand requests for help.

On July 7, 2005, four young men – all under the age of 30 – detonated bombs across London's transport system, killing themselves and more than fifty people, while injuring hundreds more. The attacks, tied to Muslim extremists, set off a wave of fear and anxiety throughout the country and exacerbated racial tensions.

Over the years, Mohammed has performed virtually every role at MYH.

What did this act of terrorism mean for the tens of thousands of Muslim youth living normal, everyday lives in the U.K.? "Young Muslims feel very much on edge. They feel they need to constantly apologize," comments Mohammed Mamdani, the 22-year-old founder of the Muslim Youth Helpline, a telephone counseling service that responds to the needs of thousands of young Muslim men and women in the U.K. each year. "We're made to feel somehow responsible."

Most disturbing to Mohammed in the days and weeks after the attack was the exclusion of Muslim youth from political and policy discussions concerning what the nation should do next. "We feel we're the subject of discussion, yet no one is interested in hearing what young Muslims have to say about the subject," notes Mohammed.

Mohammed was better prepared than most to deal with the emotional and psychological fallout of the attacks. Still, the news was devastating. For more than three years, MYH's trained peer counselors had helped young Muslims address and overcome a host of issues ranging from cultural conflicts to drug abuse and depression. While MYH's services would be needed now more than ever before, the situation facing the nation's Muslim youth had seriously deteriorated.

According to Mohammed, recent events have added the label of "home-grown terrorists" to an already disaffected community trying to define its role in British society. Young people have been particularly sensitive to this negativity, he says, adding more pressure to the social and cultural complexities of growing up as a minority in a dramatically different culture.

Mohammed recognizes that social alienation is largely to blame for the emergence of young Muslim extremists, and that the reaction to the attacks would only fuel feelings of social exclusion. "If we continue to be fragmented as a society, if we do not reengage with marginalized young people, we will never succeed in confronting the security risk," Mohammed explains. "However, reengaging with young people means listening to their concerns, and this is something those in positions of authority don't seem to consider a priority."

Listening and responding to the needs of young Muslims, on the other hand, is exactly what MYH was founded to do.

Starting Out

During his teenage years, Mohammed grew increasingly sensitive to the challenges facing Britain's largest minority group. He also knew that there were few places Muslim youth could go for support in dealing with a range of issues, from bullying at school to conflicts at home, and from issues regarding sexuality to questions concerning personal identity and cultural values.

At 18, Mohammed, a trained peer counselor, took steps to meet this critical need. In August 2001, after six months of research, Mohammed launched MYH from his bedroom at home. With his father covering the cost of a training course and a phone line, Mohammed started MYH with little more than some folders and a telephone. After just a few weeks, news of the free, confidential telephone counseling service spread, and Mohammed found himself frequently interrupting meals to take calls.

Mohammed started MYH with little more than some folders and a telephone.

Among MYH's first callers was a 16-year-old heroin addict whose parents had kicked him out of the house, and who was frequently getting into trouble with the police. Over the course of two years, Mohammed regularly counseled this youth – on the phone and in person – providing emotional support and help accessing educational and employment resources. Today, this same young man credits the helpline with empowering him to make healthier, drug-free life choices.

Building a Reputation

Since its humble beginnings, MYH has helped thousands of other youth to overcome obstacles and live richer, fuller lives. MYH now operates out of a three-room office in the bustling West Hampstead neighborhood of north London. Trained helpline volunteers answer email inquiries and calls from 6:00 P.M. to midnight, Monday through Friday, and from noon to midnight on weekends. In less than four years, MYH has responded to more than ten thousand requests for help and trained over eighty youth volunteers in counseling skills. Its reach has expanded from greater London to communities throughout the U.K., where young people hear about it through social service agencies, schools, mosques, and youth centers. A new, web-based initiative, Muslimyouth.net, attracts more than four thousand visitors per month.

In recognition of its role, MYH has received growing attention in the media, along with numerous awards. In 2003, it was honored with America Online's Innovation in the Community Award, and in 2004 the organization received the *Muslim News* Award for Excellence in Community Development. Also in that year, Mohammed was recognized by Whitbread PLC, the leading hospitality company in the U.K., as one of its Young Achievers.

Mohammed meets with MYH staff to discuss client cases and the administration of the helpline.

Mohammed receives the BT and Telephone Helplines Association 2003 Helpline Volunteer of the Year Award from Baroness Valerie Howarth.

Over the years, Mohammed, whose parents immigrated to the U.K. from East Africa and whose grandparents came from India, has performed virtually every function at MYH, including serving on its board of directors. In mid-2005, however, following a semester abroad in Egypt, he decided it was time to let "a new generation of young people lead the charity." While he continues to advise MYH's management, Mohammed hopes to pursue his passion for social justice and minority rights at the international level while completing an undergraduate degree in Arabic at Oxford University.

"The problems facing young Muslims in the U.K. are similar to those endured by minority communities across the world," he says. "As global citizens, it is our duty to engage and share ideas internationally."

Listening and Responding to Youth Needs

MYH bases its approach on the notion that young people feel more comfortable and better understood when relating to their peers. Its counseling staff comprises fifty trained volunteers, 80 percent of whom are under 25, with some as young as 18. Among them, they speak more than ten languages, allowing them to respond to the growing number of calls they receive from refugees and asylum seekers from conflict-ridden countries like Afghanistan, Iraq, and Somalia. Roughly 60

percent of Muslims living in the U.K. come from the Indian subcontinent, explains Mohammed, with the remainder coming from Europe, Africa, and the Middle East.

A philosophy of active youth participation permeates the organization's work. "Everything at MYH can be traced to the efforts of a young person," says Mohammed, adding that the organization's first website was built by a 17-year-old and its first successful grant application was drafted by an 18-year-old.

For Mohammed, volunteering provides "an important opportunity to instill good citizenship and the value of positive contribution among young Muslims." Through engaging Muslim youth as volunteers, MYH provides a much-needed service, while challenging prevailing stereotypes of Muslims as radical extremists. Instead, it offers a powerful illustration of the positive impact of Muslim youth in the wider community.

Says Mohammed, "MYH's message is of hard-working young Muslims who have overcome cultural and social conflicts, as well as a climate of intolerance and negativity, to promote a cause that has improved the lives of thousands of young people."

Muslim youth find out about the helpline through posters and flyers distributed to schools and colleges, youth agencies and police stations. From a specially designated call-in room, MYH-trained counselors respond to a range of youth needs. Roughly a third of callers seek help concerning relationships and sexuality; another third suffer from depression and suicidal thoughts. The remainder seek advice in dealing with verbal and physical abuse, homelessness, education and employment needs, and issues related to their religion.

According to Layli Uddin, who coordinates and oversees MYH volunteers, one of the biggest factors contributing to the inner conflicts young Muslims face is "parental oppression." Such tension stems from parents' expectations of what they want their children to be (mainly doctors or lawyers), and the degree to which their children conform to cultural values and traditions, such as arranged marriages. Mohammed tells the story of one 17-year-old female who ran away from home to escape what she considered to be a repressive environment in which she couldn't go out with friends or pursue her interests. The girl knew that eventually she would be expected to agree to an arranged marriage. MYH counselors ended up holding a mediation session between the girl and her parents, with both parties compromising their stand in favor of maintaining strong family bonds.

Sometimes, the very act of seeking help is considered taboo. Within Muslim culture, for example, depression can be perceived as a weakness of faith, Layli explains. Admitting that you are depressed could be an indication that you "don't believe in God enough," she adds.

Issues such as homosexuality and premarital relationships are also "impossible to talk about within Muslim communities," says Mohammed, which contributes even further to the anxiety and sense of isolation experienced by Muslim youth.

Indeed, MYH has at times been criticized for its role in counseling young people experiencing conflict over their sexual identity. "It's an emotive and controversial subject," explains Mohammed, "particularly when families and communities get involved. Our service is non-chastising, and we prefer to concentrate on dealing with the issues and exploring the options available to a young Muslim in that situation."

Training Helpline Volunteers

To ensure that they have what it takes to address a range of caller needs, helpline volunteers undergo a rigorous selection and training process. Candidates first submit a formal application. An extensive interview and background checks follow. Those who make it through this initial screening attend twelve in-depth training sessions, including modules on Islamic counseling skills, substance abuse, mental health, relationships, sexuality, and email counseling. Upon successful completion of the training, the work of volunteers is closely monitored during a three-month trial period. At all times, a supervisor, who holds an accredited qualification in counseling, is on hand to field questions and offer advice.

Roughly a third of callers seek help concerning relationships and sexuality; another third suffer from depression and suicidal thoughts.

Mohammed congratulates a runner who raised money for MYH during the 2004 British 10K Road Race through central London.

Volunteers are introduced to the array of social problems faced by young Muslims and encouraged to explore their own attitudes and perceptions related to race, gender, and cultural issues.

Helpline volunteers commit to spending a minimum of three hours per week counseling their peers. Every call and email is logged on a "record" sheet. While MYH offers an anonymous, confidential service, clients are asked, when appropriate, for a pseudonym to use in place of their real name, and for basic personal data such as age, ethnicity, and location. Helpline volunteers also record the nature of the caller's concern and the type of support provided. Such information is used to track each client's progress and to monitor the program's overall effectiveness.

Far from prescribing answers, helpline volunteers are trained as skilled listeners, who guide and encourage callers to develop solutions that work for them. During a typical call, a counselor will listen to and reassure the caller, gaining trust and exploring whatever challenges the caller faces. The counselor will then engage the caller in identifying various solutions and developing a plan of action. The call concludes with the caller committing to take a step toward resolution of his or her problem. Roughly 70 percent of callers call back, with approximately 10 percent agreeing to face-to-face meetings – "befriending visits" – held off-site.

Launching Muslimyouth.net

The sister organization that MYH launched in 2004, Muslimyouth.net, is an online initiative designed to complement MYH's existing services, while expanding its reach. The site highlights issues facing Muslim youth, targeting young people who may be reluctant to call or send an email to MYH. It offers a comprehensive directory of support services for Muslim youth, relevant news items, an events calendar, and a forum for online dialogue. In the weeks following the July 2005 terrorist attacks, for example, visitors to the site were polled about their reactions to the bombings and the events that followed. Young people also had the opportunity to share their thoughts and feelings through the site's discussion forum.

Emphasis on the site is placed not only on challenges facing Muslim youth, but also on their achievements and contributions to the community. In addition, in-depth feature stories explore topics such as education, addiction, sexuality, citizenship, and identity.

Muslimyouth.net's staff of twenty volunteers ranges in age from 16 to 25. To prepare for their roles, volunteers complete a short course in writing skills, attend an audio-visual workshop, and train in editing and moderating online forums. They are also introduced to the array of social problems faced by young Muslims and encouraged to explore their own attitudes and perceptions related to race, gender, and cultural issues.

To spotlight urgent and unmet needs in the community, the website features a new campaign every three months. One recent campaign focused on the lives of Muslim youth who have run away from home and currently live in the streets. Another campaign focused on the situation of imprisoned Muslim youth. To help these young offenders feel less alone – and forgotten – more than a thousand received small gifts and messages from the Muslimyouth.net community. "The response we received from these youth was overwhelmingly positive," says Layli, adding that a future campaign will focus on the adult prison population.

Planning for the Future

Deeply saddened and disturbed by the anti-Muslim sentiment that exists in today's world, Mohammed holds tight to the hope that such attitudes can be transformed, particularly through better meeting the needs of Muslim youth; through engaging them in the policy-making process; through strengthening community ties across cultures; and through providing alternative messages to those offered by the mainstream media.

In the future, he would like to see the MYH model adapted to other countries – both in the West and the Muslim world. "It [MYH] would work almost perfectly in Western countries with minority Muslim communities and play an important role in ensuring that young Muslims are engaged and not isolated," he says.

While MYH focuses on meeting the needs of Muslim youth, Mohammed emphasizes an even larger message in its work – the vital importance in today's world of serving others, understanding differences, and recognizing our shared humanity.

"Through MYH, I seek to make peace with the world that I live in," says Mohammed, "and propagate my belief in selflessness and service and my hope that one day this can become a shared value among all citizens of the world." ∎

Created in 2004, Muslimyouth.net complements MYH's existing services, highlighting issues facing Muslim youth and providing valuable resources.

"Whitbread Young Achievers Awards aim to recognize and celebrate outstanding volunteers who strive to make change. Mohammed is an inspirational example of what the youth of today can achieve. Mixing passion and dedication with the highest level of commitment and genuine hard work, he managed to build the trust and support of his peers to bridge the generation gap within his community. His reward was to make a real difference to hundreds of lives."

Alan Parker
Chief Executive Officer Whitbread PLC
Luton, England

ADVICE FROM MOHAMMED ON:

Developing a Youth Counseling Service

- **Identify existing services and areas of need.** Mohammed spent six months researching youth needs and planning how best to address them before testing his ideas during a pilot phase launched from his home.

- **Form a team made up of like-minded individuals.** "Never go it alone," says Mohammed, most of whose friends have volunteered with MYH at one point.

- **Make sure volunteers are well trained.** Mohammed underwent extensive training prior to his first role as a helpline volunteer. Today, MYH places a premium on screening and training its volunteers to ensure the quality of its services. To address client needs that exceed the experience and expertise of helpline volunteers, MYH engages the support of trained psychologists and specialist agencies.

- **Above all, maintain the confidentiality and privacy of your clients.** MYH maintains detailed records of its clients' concerns and proposed responses, all of which are kept confidential. Such records help the organization track its progress and refine its approaches.

- **Collaborate with other youth-serving organizations.** Over time, MYH has developed relationships with a number of Muslim organizations that share a similar mission and offer complementary services.

- **Invest in the people you work with.** "Motivate them. Commend them and inspire action through your example," says Mohammed. "Learn to smile, even when the going gets tough. It'll keep up morale among your coworkers."

- **Develop systems for monitoring and evaluating the service you provide.** "Most people forget how important it is to measure your results," cautions Mohammed. "Every organization needs to be able to demonstrate its effectiveness with hard evidence, especially if you are to access more funding."

MUHAMED MEŠIĆ

Communicating a message of peace through politics

BOSNIA AND HERZEGOVINA

The Balkans have seen their fair share of troubles and hardships during the last years, having moved from a time of dictators into a time of thieves. Particularly in Bosnia, where many wounds are still open, young people seem to bridge all gaps with most ease. I believe that the only way the country can function is when young people – with pure hearts and fresh ideas – get into politics. There's a saying in Bosnia that young people don't have any 'hidden nuts in their pockets,' meaning young people in politics don't have dubious backgrounds or secrets to hide. The new generation must gain a foothold in government and politics – the sooner the better – since there's not much time left. Slowly but steadily, I believe we're on the way.

– Muhamed Mešić

Muhamed meets with members of a local youth group.

SECTION TWO
Different Roads to the Same Destination: **A Better World**

Muhamed joins former Finnish president Martti Ahtisaari in a panel discussion at the second annual Balkan Youth Forum.

Muhamed Mešić was just 8 years old in 1992, when war broke out in the former Yugoslavia and the republic of Bosnia and Herzegovina declared its independence. For three years, his hometown of Tuzla, a prominent industrial center in northeastern Bosnia, lay under siege by Serb forces seeking to take control of the multiethnic city. The bloody civil war resulted in the deaths of more than two hundred thousand people, with more than a million displaced from their homes.

Not long after the war broke out, Muhamed narrowly escaped being killed when a mortar attack destroyed the temporary school he attended in a basement near his family's apartment. The attack came less than a minute after his teacher had dismissed class.

"That was when I realized life has meaning," recalls Muhamed, who refers to that day as his second birthday. Now 20, the tall, lanky idealist has put the war behind him. Of all the lessons the war taught him, the most important was the power of love.

Driven by a dream of a better Bosnia, Muhamed currently serves as the youngest-ever city councilor in Tuzla, a position to which he was elected in 2004. Through his role, Muhamed hopes to be part of a wave of young leaders he envisions asserting themselves in the Bosnian political landscape, which many citizens view as a minefield of corruption and cronyism. With his boyish face, t-shirt, and backpack, Muhamed's image stands in stark contrast to that of your average politician. It's not uncommon for senior citizens to stop him on the street with a word of thanks for his fresh optimism.

> *Through his role, Muhamed hopes to be part of a wave of young leaders he envisions asserting themselves in the Bosnian political landscape, which many citizens view as a minefield of corruption and cronyism.*

Asked why he's chosen to engage in politics at such a young age, Muhamed responds, "We're raising our hand to the enemies of the future." Among those enemies he identifies are poverty, hatred, violence, and ethnic intolerance. Through advocating policies designed to stimulate economic growth, address social injustice, and better meet youth needs, Muhamed hopes to avert future crises in this conflict-prone region.

Achieving Social Good through Public Service

For Muhamed, positive change can happen only when people believe a better future is possible. The legacy of the past has contributed to widespread pessimism among Bosnian citizens, he points out. Almost in spite of the past, Muhamed retains a hopeful outlook and a hunger for the kind of knowledge and understanding that will make him a more enlightened public servant.

At a time when many Bosnian youth dream of leaving their country in search of greater opportunity abroad, Muhamed has remained steadfast in his commitment to stay.

Maintaining an expansive worldview is critical to being an effective leader, asserts Muhamed, an avid reader who travels whenever he can afford to. Long fascinated by other cultures, he speaks eighteen languages – including Kiswahili, Hindi, and Hebrew. An ardent flag collector, he's as passionate about people getting in touch with their own cultural identity as he is about instilling values of our shared global humanity. "You can be this or that," notes Muhamed of cultural, ethnic, and national differences, "but in the end you're always human. I've always looked at the globe as one."

Muhamed views public service – and his involvement in political life – as a critical pathway to achieve the goals of greater justice and a better future for Tuzla's citizens. He came to his job of city councilor after serving for four years as youth advisor to the mayor of Tuzla. (Then, as it does now, his age distinguished him. At the time, he was the youngest advisor to an elected official in Europe.) In his advisory role, he counseled the mayor on youth policies and issues related to education, employment, and how to go about fostering peace and understanding among the city's diverse population of 165,000. Much of his work focused on celebrating the energy and talents of young people and restoring a sense of civic pride among Tuzla's citizens.

At a time when many Bosnian youth dream of leaving their country in search of greater opportunity abroad, Muhamed has remained steadfast in his commitment to stay. His affection for the city is reflected in the "I Love Tuzla" campaign that he helped forge through the mayor's office. "We want to make people proud of Tuzla," he says, adding that the campaign is about transformation and positive change. In overcoming the divisive legacy of the past, Muhamed collaborated with city officials to promote global values based on peace and cooperation. With his encouragement, a bust of Martin Luther King Jr. was installed on a prominent street corner near the mayor's office.

Muhamed addresses a crowd during his election campaign.

Working within the System

At first opposed to the idea of running for elective office, Muhamed grew intrigued when approached by the Social Democratic Party, which he says is known for its inclusiveness, tough stance on corruption, and promotion of social justice. "At first it seemed like the wrong thing at the wrong time," comments Muhamed on his election bid, "but then it became clear to me that fighting for justice was even easier if done from a place where you're put by the people to listen to them, and where your role is to do your best in making their lives better." As it turned out, of the more than two hundred candidates to run in the municipal elections that year, Muhamed was the third most popular when the votes were tallied.

While serving as youth advisor to Tuzla's mayor, Muhamed contributed to efforts to clean up the Pannonian Lake, a former swamp now visited by more than one hundred thousand people each year.

As city councilor, Muhamed is responsible for identifying, assessing, and proposing solutions to the problems facing local citizens, particularly those living in the poorer, western portion of Tuzla where Muhamed grew up and continues to live with his family.

If there's one aspect of his current job that Muhamed values most, it's the chance to listen to, learn from, and serve Tuzla's citizens. Even while campaigning, Muhamed says, he enjoyed meeting and talking with a wide array of constituents – young and old, housewives and business leaders, students and unemployed people – about their needs and hopes for the future. Today, much of his time is spent gauging public opinion on existing or proposed local policies.

If there's one aspect of his current job that Muhamed values most, it's the chance to listen to, learn from, and serve Tuzla's citizens.

Among his accomplishments, Muhamed has succeeded in attracting greater foreign investment to the city, and with it more jobs. He's also proud of an initiative he helped to launch in which city employees, including himself, donated a portion of their wages to help victims of the December 2004 tsunami in Asia. Currently, he's focused on enacting measures that will prevent brushfires in Ilincica, an ancient forest and popular hiking destination just north of the city.

Muhamed admits that his job can be physically and mentally draining, especially given that he divides his time between Tuzla and Vienna, Austria, where he's pursuing a law degree. Gaining closure on important issues can be a painstaking process, he says, recounting a recent episode when council members engaged in a policy debate that lasted from 9 A.M. until 1 A.M. the next day. Still, he cherishes his new role. "It's simply cool. Every day I get approached by both young and old people on the street, either commending what I've said at council meetings or what the city has done. That's reward in itself."

So what's Muhamed's long-term vision? While he doesn't dwell too much on the future, there's talk of his becoming mayor of Tuzla some day. ■

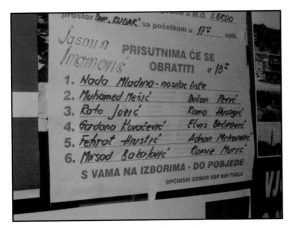

Of his role as Tuzla's youngest-ever city councilor, Muhamed says, "It's simply cool."

"*Peace is far more than the resolution of conflict and absence of war. True peace can only be achieved when there is peace within us and peace among us. The World Youth Peace Summit brings together dynamic youth leaders who share the dream of peace. Muhamed Mešić is one of those leaders. Through his values, work, and example, he helps nurture peace not only in his native Bosnia and Herzegovina, but throughout the world.*"

Bawa Jain
Chairman World Youth Peace Summit
New York, New York, United States

"*While obstacles abound – political, social, economic – this may be one of the most exciting times to be young in the history of the Balkans. Civil society organizations have emerged to address the needs of children and youth – many of them led by extremely able, visionary young people. These young adults are creative, enterprising, forward thinking, and persistent. They've grown up talking about – and acting on – their political and social convictions. Now they are co-architects of today's civil society, eager to contribute to new structures and craving the knowledge that will help them to do so.*"

Martti Ahtisaari
Former President Finland
Chair Crisis Management Initiative
Chair Balkan Children and Youth Foundation
Helsinki, Finland

ADVICE FROM MUHAMED ON:

Engaging in Politics

- **Build a track record as someone who cares about local issues and who exhibits leadership in addressing challenges.** Muhamed admits that he never actively pursued a career in politics, but ended up engaging in public service as a result of his desire to contribute to positive change. His involvement in the community started in his late teens, when he co-founded "Youth of Tuzla," a youth association that has undertaken a variety of community projects, including producing a play, renovating an abandoned park, and helping the elderly.

- **Expand your worldview**. Muhamed is careful to read widely and network with people outside his city and country to keep his ideas fresh and his mind open to multiple perspectives.

- **Be able to back up your proposals and assertions with hard facts and research.** Earn people's respect through your passion and knowledge, says Muhamed.

- **Be a good listener.** Muhamed spends hours each week talking with – and especially listening to – Tuzla's citizens about issues in their lives and current and proposed policies.

- **Tell your story well.** Learn to advocate for your beliefs through speaking passionately, from the heart. Whether you're addressing a special-interest group, the general public, or the media, stay focused on your key messages.

- **Be persistent.** Says Muhamed, "Being successful requires a lot of knocking on doors and convincing those in authority to let you succeed. If they don't trust you, you need to build up a big fire, a big coalition. United we stand; divided we fall."

- **Don't be ashamed of your ideas.** Muhamed declares, "There's no such thing as a bad idea when it's about helping people and making the future a better one!"

JULIA PARSHINA

Reaching out to child victims of a nuclear disaster

RUSSIA

I was inspired by watching a TV program about children who suffered as a result of the Chernobyl nuclear disaster. I wanted to show these children that they are important, that their lives are no less valuable because of their health problems. They are just children, and children need love and attention, so I tried to give it to them because they don't always get it from their families and society.

Julia enjoys working with children and is studying to be a teacher.

After the project, I realized that young people all over the world can change the society around them. To make positive changes, you don't have to do a great many things. At the beginning, it's enough to unglue your body from the sofa that stands in front of the TV and look around.

– Julia Parshina

SECTION TWO

Different Roads to the Same Destination: **A Better World**

On April 26, 1986, an explosion at the Chernobyl nuclear power plant in what was then the Soviet Union caused what would become the world's worst nuclear accident. For ten days, a fire spewed tons of toxic materials into the atmosphere, with radioactive substances carried by wind and rain into large areas of Belarus, Russia, and Ukraine. A 1995 United Nations report estimated that three to four million children were directly or indirectly affected by the disaster, some of whom suffer today from congenital birth deformities and increased rates of cancer and leukemia.

In the fall of 2003, Julia Parshina, a 19-year-old college student, saw a TV program describing the lives of children who were growing up physically and mentally disabled as a result of the accident. "The stories about their lives touched my heart, and I decided my friends and I should help them somehow and change their lives for the better," recalls Julia.

A few months after viewing that TV show, Julia and several of her friends conceived of a summer camp program to offer recreational and artistic activities to young victims of the disaster. Because such children often grow up feeling isolated –

AP Photo/Efrem Lukatsky

People light candles at a monument dedicated to the victims of the Chernobyl nuclear disaster.

with low self-confidence and poorly developed social skills – the summer camp would provide opportunities for them to interact with youth volunteers while boosting the children's self-esteem and sense of belonging.

"The stories about their lives touched my heart, and I decided my friends and I should help them somehow and change their lives for the better," recalls Julia.

Julia's motivation for starting the camp was driven by two important needs. First, she sought "to help children to socialize in our world and to make their lives better and brighter." A second goal was to demonstrate to young volunteers that they "are able to change the world and it's enough to have a strong wish to do it."

According to Julia, many young people where she lives want to contribute to their community, but few organizations exist to help them. "There are a lot of young people who don't know how to use their free time and don't know how to develop a project," she says.

Transforming an Idea into a Reality

While Chernobyl is located in Ukraine, more than four hundred miles southwest of Julia's home city of Voronezh, she discovered that a number of child victims of the disaster were receiving treatment nearby, at the Barkova Gora sanatorium. To get their project off the ground, she and a group of her peers contacted the manager of the sanatorium to offer their support, and they were pleasantly surprised when their proposal was accepted.

Julia attributes her success to both her own stubborn streak and the encouragement of her parents, who were happy to see their only child take on a project dedicated to helping others.

Securing the modest financial resources the group needed for their project wasn't easy, remembers the red-haired Julia, an A-student who enjoys swimming, skiing, and taking part in archaeological expeditions. She attributes her success to both her own stubborn streak and the encouragement of her parents, who were happy to see their only child take on a project dedicated to helping others. When the government rejected the group's initial request for financial assistance, Julia learned

about a small grants program offered by the New Perspectives Foundation, a nongovernmental organization in Moscow that empowers Russian youth to play an active role in democracy building. Julia's group applied and received a grant of approximately U.S.$1,000.

With the grant award, Julia and her peers were able to purchase supplies and organize transportation for the children and volunteers to and from the sanatorium and various activities scheduled in other locations. The group's work was made somewhat easier through embedding their project within the Patriotic Camp Tanais, a summer camp that Julia and many of her fellow volunteers had attended for many years. With their access to the camp's resources, the group was able to offer participating children the chance to swim in the Tanais River and enjoy nature in the surrounding forest.

Before officially launching the camp's activities, Julia took time to identify the individual skills and interests of the twenty young people who volunteered to participate in the program. As she is studying at Voronezh State Pedagogical University to be a teacher, Julia was able to provide basic training to the volunteers in how to lead classes and engage children with special needs.

Camp volunteers prepare to offer a class in nail art.

Finally, the volunteers split into groups, or clubs, each offering different activities ranging from therapeutic games to craft projects including origami, nail art, batik, and clay modeling. Although at first a number of volunteers were nervous when interacting with the children with special needs, their anxiety quickly wore off. While lacking in experience, they learned by listening to their hearts, says Julia.

During one group exercise, participants gathered in a circle and took off their shoes. Next, each had to put on a pair of shoes as fast as they could, irrespective of whether the shoes matched. Through the game, the children learned to make swift hand movements, which helps to stimulate their mental functioning, Julia explains. During June of 2004, clubs met once a day for ten days, with the experience culminating in an art exhibition of participants' work.

Julia and her fellow volunteers organize an evening of entertainment during the last night of the camp.

At the conclusion of their first summer camp, Julia and the other volunteers were deeply encouraged by the results. "We couldn't recognize the children," she says. "They had changed from unhappy pessimists to being more satisfied with themselves. . . . Now, they believe that although they are a little bit different, they are equal to other people."

Giving and Receiving

The volunteers benefited as much as the children themselves. Through reaching out to children in need, they experienced the inner rewards of making a difference in others' lives. They also developed greater understanding of, and empathy for, those who are different; and they acquired valuable skills, such as how to work as a team, communicate effectively, set goals, and overcome obstacles. In the process, they developed greater confidence in their abilities and a clearer sense of their gifts.

"We couldn't recognize the children," says Julia. "They had changed from unhappy pessimists to being more satisfied with themselves."

According to Vera Martynenko, director of Iskra, a children's organization in Voronezh, projects such as Julia's are important for developing young people's social consciousness. "Participation in volunteer projects prevents youth from being indifferent to other people's problems and teaches them to identify weaknesses in their community and to find ways to ease social pains," she says.

During its second year, in 2005, the camp attracted more than thirty volunteers, with the group having expanded its efforts to another treatment facility. Adults from the Voronezh area are calling in to see how they can get involved, and not only has the city's minister of education voiced his approval of the team's work, but several local government offices have offered their support.

Although she has only one year of college left before pursuing a career as an English teacher, Julia expects the summer camp program to continue on.

Through her experience, Julia has come to value the importance of "thinking globally" while "acting locally." "I realized that to address global problems, people should start by solving small, local, but no less important problems," she says.

While generating greater public awareness and civic involvement in addressing children's needs is a key goal of her efforts, Julia emphasizes that "the most fulfilling part of this work is the smiles on the children's faces. At such moments, I realize the main purpose of our lives is to help others. I'm sure even a million dollars cannot substitute for this feeling of satisfaction." ∎

The Chernobyl plant is now closed, but Julia and her fellow volunteers continue to address its legacy.

"In an age when we honor heroes, dedicate monuments, and declare world heritage sites, I want to celebrate the real treasure of human life: our children. The sum of one child's possibilities, ambitions, dreams, energy, and innocence is enough to literally change the world. Adults are often amazed that our young people are so brave, so selfless in the work they do to help others. Children are the kindhearted messengers of a brighter tomorrow . . . the future looks very bright."

Muhammad Ali
First three-time World Heavyweight Champion
United Nations Messenger of Peace
Berrien Springs, Michigan, United States

ADVICE FROM JULIA ON:

Starting a Volunteer Project

- **Form a team of committed volunteers.** Julia started out by engaging close friends and fellow college students in her efforts. Later, she distributed information about the project at local high schools and universities.

- **Train volunteers in the basic skills they need.** With an academic background in education and child development, Julia was able to provide volunteers with basic training in how to deliver lessons in the arts and how to address special learning needs.

- **Develop materials that describe your project.** To describe her project to potential volunteers, the media, and donors, Julia developed basic materials (e.g., a one-page flyer). Such materials can be inexpensive to produce – she used colored paper and a photocopying machine – and are extremely helpful as you conduct basic outreach.

- **Target the media to get your story told.** Julia worked hard and experienced a number of rejections before reporters would take her project seriously. Her persistence eventually paid off, with local radio and TV outlets now receptive to featuring occasional stories about the group's work and assisting in volunteer recruitment efforts through broadcasting brief announcements.

- **Approach diverse sources for funding.** Julia's initial efforts to generate government funding for her project failed, but eventually she learned of a foundation that supported youth volunteer efforts. Now that her project has a track record, she has succeeded in obtaining funds from local government offices, as well as individual contributions from business representatives.

- **Network with like-minded groups and organizations.** Julia urges those who are launching a social project to talk to others in their local community and region who are working on similar issues.

- **Encourage your team.** Julia is careful to acknowledge the special contributions of team members and thank them for their participation.

KRITAYA SREESUNPAGIT

Creating opportunities for youth to get involved in their communities

THAILAND

The only way to answer the question about the meaning of life is to live the question. I still do not know what I want to achieve, but I am learning every day. Having a chance to search for who you are and what you believe in, and to try out your ideas, is the best way to learn. There are so many problems in our society that it is difficult to identify the most important ones. You cannot wait for someone else to address those issues. It is up to every one of us to take notice of what is going on, search for solutions, and most important of all, take action.

– Kritaya Sreesunpagit

Through her "I'MPOSSIBLE" campaigns, Kritaya recruits Thai youth to develop their own community-based projects.

Making volunteering fun and exciting is a key goal of Kritaya's organization.

YIY provides hundreds of youth with opportunities to find out for themselves how to make a difference in their communities.

A group of young people in a large shopping mall in downtown Bangkok drift over to an exhibition of posters by local artists, attracted by the lively music of "Playground" and "Morning Surfers" – two popular Thai bands. On an adjacent stage (located between a McDonald's and a Starbucks), a group of young activists speak to the growing crowd about the need to get involved in their communities, even inviting some of the onlookers to come up on stage to participate in a skit. The event also offers videos of well-known artists and musicians encouraging young people to become more active.

The multimedia event, called the I'MPOSSIBLE fair, is designed to attract young people of different levels of interest. Those youth who are inspired to volunteer approach a booth where they can sign up to participate in community activities, while others with experience and a specific volunteer project in mind can go to another booth to apply for a small grant. A young woman at a third stand calls on passing shoppers to support a "seed fund" for youth volunteer activities by buying t-shirts and other products. Donors are encouraged to go to the organization's website (www. deksiam.com) to track the progress of the programs they are supporting.

The two-day fair was organized by YIY (Youth Innovation Year), the nonprofit organization that Kritaya Sreesunpagit and a few of her friends founded in 2003. Its goal is to mobilize young people to volunteer, and to ensure they have the tools and experience to be successful. The March 2005 event in the shopping mall, funded through the Thai Health Promotion Foundation and UNICEF, mobilized eighty youth to sign up as volunteers and demonstrates Kritaya's creative flair for making volunteering fun.

Kritaya, 26, recognizes that while some young people know exactly what they want to accomplish in life, others need more time and guidance to explore their path to action. As the director of YIY, she provides hundreds of youth with opportunities to find out for themselves how to make a difference in their communities. "Young people are generally energetic, creative, and most of all they search for passion, trying to understand themselves and society," she says. "For them to put their ideas into practice, they need to learn innovative ways to solve problems, and [they] benefit greatly from the learning process."

Although she was born in Bangkok, Kritaya spent her early years in Canberra, Australia, where her father worked in the Thai embassy. It was not until she returned to Thailand, and began attending Thammasat University in Bangkok, that Kritaya got her first chance to explore the answer "to the biggest question of all – what I wanted to achieve in life." A two-month stay in a rural village in northern Thailand provided a first step – exposing her to the deep poverty of the region and, in particular, to the rural population's lack of access to the world of information technology. She decided to do something to address the problem.

During her final year at the university, Kritaya and a friend, Sunit Shrestha, launched Thai RuralNet, a small organization aimed at using information technology to empower those living in underserved, rural areas. Thai RuralNet places a particular focus on combining traditional and scientific knowledge to ensure greater productivity among poor farmers. "We took on a huge challenge," Kritaya says, "and succeeded in using relevant information technology to improve people's livelihood opportunities." She submitted the project to the World Bank's Development Marketplace "Innovation Competition" and won financial support to carry out the project. Perhaps more important, she says, was the fact that "this project gave us a chance to learn valuable lessons from our mistakes." That experience – of trying something new, learning through practice, and mobilizing funding to support the project – changed her life, Kritaya explains, adding, "We wanted to create that same opportunity for other young people."

Kritaya recognized a real need for an organization in Thailand that would encourage young people to think creatively about how to improve their communities. In founding such an organization – YIY – she wanted to give youth a chance to experiment, and to convince them that it is normal, even fashionable, to get involved in their communities. But Kritaya was also aware of the obstacles standing in the way.

In Thailand, as in many countries, youth often tend to view service to the community as "uncool," she explains, or as demanding too much personal sacrifice or loyalty to a cause. Most parents do not support the idea of joining the nonprofit sector, preferring for their sons and daughters to take more high-paying, prestigious career paths. One of the most difficult barriers to overcome, Kritaya believes, is that the majority of Thai people do not feel a deep personal responsibility to actively address the social problems around them.

Growing up in a period of rapid change, Thai youth are surrounded by shopping malls, TV ads, and the Internet – all promoting a lifestyle often beyond their reach. Traditional and religious values are frequently at odds with this increasingly consumer-oriented culture. Kritaya sees her challenge as answering the question, How do you mobilize today's young people to play an active role in society?

This group of young people received YIY grants for their community projects in 2003.

Kritaya speaks at the opening of the Youth Innovation Fair, held in Bangkok to promote young people's positive engagement in their communities.

Providing Skills to Young Volunteers

YIY gives young people who have innovative, creative ideas about how to improve society the support they need to try them out. Participation offers a chance for youth to develop themselves, explore their ideas about how to work for social change, and leave with both the confidence and the funding "to make something happen." YIY works with local organizations that already have established positive relations with young people and that have high ethical standards.

In addition to holding regular training camps on how to develop a "social venture" and matching up young activists with adult mentors in related fields, YIY has a grant-making program, Youth Innovation Marketplace (YIM), to fund the most innovative ideas. Young people compete for the grants, which are evaluated for their creativity, commitment, sustainability, social importance, and impact. To date, YIY has funded seventeen such volunteer projects, with budgets ranging from 50,000 to 400,000 baht (up to about U.S.$9,500). Among the winners so far: an antipollution campaign to clean up a river, an exchange program among culturally isolated youth from different regions of the country, and a project to restore mangrove farms.

As part of a program to improve farming techniques, YIY volunteers work with rural farmers to help make organic fertilizer.

The programs, organized by independent youth groups all over Thailand, are active in such cities as Bangkok, Chiang Mai, and Buriram. Some of the projects, however, engage disadvantaged youth in poor, rural areas. From five to twenty youth participate in each project, working together to develop a range of volunteer activities, from environmental initiatives to small business enterprises. Kritaya keeps the various groups in contact so they can learn from each other, often through the YIY website and CD-ROMs. YIY also puts participants in direct contact with potential funders and helps them with publicity and the media, ensuring that they have the capacity to continue independently.

Turning Dreams into Reality

YIY has used a number of creative strategies to mobilize young people, including a "Youth Social Entrepreneur Camp" held in Bangkok in 2003 that attracted thirty youth. In addition to workshops and activities that equipped participants with the skills to plan and carry out a volunteer project, the camp helped participants to write funding proposals for submission to YIM.

One volunteer effort inspired by the camp experience resulted in the building of a library at a small, impoverished school in northeastern Thailand. The project, which received 337,500 baht (approximately U.S.$8,000), was organized by Fai, a shy girl who attended the training session. "I had no idea at the time I participated in the Social Entrepreneurs Camp what project to do," admits Fai. "But as soon as I got back home I told my friends, and we came up with this project." In addition to collecting and cataloging two thousand books for the library, Fai and her colleagues trained a number of the local students to run the library once it was established.

After working for two years to ensure that other young people gain the knowledge and experience to be successful, Kritaya is now sharpening her own skills as a recipient of the prestigious Ashoka Fellowship, which is sponsored by a leading global organization that supports social entrepreneurs.

Kritaya acknowledges that youth-led volunteer initiatives do not always run smoothly. But in the end, young people learn invaluable lessons about the challenges, the successes, and the joys of contributing to society and improving people's lives. She also takes satisfaction in seeing people like Fai be transformed by the process. "From a girl who did not know what she liked, and who had a hard time communicating, Fai has become an energetic and positive leader," she states proudly.

Kritaya is determined to ensure that more young people like Fai get this unique opportunity to learn about themselves and have a lasting impact on their communities. She wants to build up YIY so that it can identify and support fifty effective programs every year. Kritaya is particularly interested in finding more fun and creative ways to inspire Thai youth to get involved. "I believe we are here to create, without which we are nothing," she says. "So this is our creation, our way to change the world from this little corner." ∎

Participants in a "dream searching" activity have posted their ideas for how to improve society on a wall.

"Youth not only represent the future, they are also agents of change today. Across the world, young people like Kritaya Sreesunpagit are working in their societies to help find lasting solutions to address problems such as poverty, hunger, social alienation, and lack of opportunity in their communities and beyond. By mobilizing youth to be drivers of social change, Kritaya and countless others like her demonstrate the importance of ensuring that the dreams, ideas, and initiatives of young people are given the space to impact the world for the better."

Mark Malloch Brown
Chief of Staff
to United Nations Secretary-General Kofi Annan
New York, New York, United States

ADVICE FROM KRITAYA ON:

Mobilizing Youth to Lead Change in Their Communities

· **Find innovative ways to get young people involved.** Recruit young people in places where they spend much of their free time. Kritaya's organization sets up booths at shopping malls, where members can sign up young people on the spot who are interested in volunteering. YIY also turns to popular rock bands and well-known celebrities to encourage young people to get active in their communities.

· **Be sure young people have the skills they need to be successful.** Kritaya places a high priority on providing young people with the skills and the experiences necessary to be successful, typically through regular workshops and training camps. YIY believes that it is only through trial and error that you can learn how to develop and run an effective program.

· **Recognize that developing leaders is as important as carrying out a successful volunteer program.** While some of the young people who decide to run a volunteer project may return to school or go on to university after a year, they have learned how satisfying it is to contribute to society. They have gained confidence in themselves and in their abilities to achieve something important. As one YIY-funded participant noted, "It is not only about making a difference for others, but also [about] how this experience changed our lives."

· **Make it fun.** Kritaya sees her organization as a "playground" for young people to develop themselves and explore their ideas about how to work for social change. The process needs to be fun, with a lot of attention given to building up young people's teamwork skills and developing friendships. Kritaya wrote a "pop" song about having the power to change the world – which ended up on the Top 40 radio charts.

For further information, visit: **www.deksiam.com**

ROTTERDAM-KRALINGEN
FREE THE CHILDREN GROUP

Increasing educational opportunities for children in Kenya

THE NETHERLANDS

Our group started one day in my sitting room. My mom and I were watching Craig [Kielburger, founder of Free The Children] on Oprah, and when I looked at my mom I saw that she was crying. So I asked, 'Mom, why are you crying?' and she told me that she was really touched by Craig and all he was doing to help other kids. 'We can help, too,' I said. And that's how our FTC group was born. Mom invited a bunch of kids we knew over to our house to talk, and it just started from there.

– Esa Kasmir

FREE THE CHILDREN
children helping children through education

*Founded in 1995,
Free The Children is an
international network
of children helping
children.*

Members of the Rotterdam-Kralingen Free The Children group include:

Tian Ci Claase

Alexandra Cohen

Frederik Groenland

Esa Kasmir

Sam Kloosterboer

Julius Rasenberg

Stijn Wilbers

OUR TIME IS NOW

Esa Kasmir was 3 when he sought to comfort his mother, who became teary-eyed after seeing on TV how one young person had mobilized thousands of others around the world to address the problem of child labor. Without Esa's encouragement, his mother might not have taken steps to gather a group of slightly older children in their neighborhood to figure out what they could do. Today, three years later, Esa is one of seven young members of the Rotterdam-Kralingen "Youth in Action" group of Free The Children, a global charitable organization headquartered in Toronto, Canada.

Free The Children was started by Craig Kielburger, who at the age of 12 read a newspaper article about a young boy in Pakistan who was murdered for speaking out against child labor. The boy, Iqbal Masih, was sold into child labor himself at the age of 4. While Craig knew nothing about child labor at the time, he immersed himself in studying the issue and gathered a group of his friends to discuss how they might help their peers. Soon afterward, they established Free The Children to liberate children around the world from abuse and exploitation, while enabling young people to recognize their role as leaders.

Free The Children is the largest network of children helping children through education in the world.

Stijn Wilbers speaks on children's rights.

Through the organization's unique, youth-driven approach, more than one million young people have been involved in innovative programs in more than forty-five countries. As a result of their efforts, in excess of four hundred primary schools have been built, medical supplies have been shipped around the world, and poor families have accessed alternative sources of income, thereby reducing the need for their children to work.

Members of the Rotterdam-Kralingen Free The Children group range from 6 to 11 years of age. They include president Stijn Wilbers, 11; vice president Tian Ci Claase, 11; treasurer Frederik Groenland, 11; Alexandra Cohen, 10; Esa Kasmir, 6; Sam Kloosterboer, 10; and Julius Rasenberg, 10. All are students at Rotterdamse School Vereniging, a semi-public school located in the center of Rotterdam, the second-largest city in the Netherlands. Serving as their mentor, Esa's mother Alisa helps with everything from orchestrating the group's Sunday meetings, which take place around her family's kitchen table, to providing transportation to and from events.

"Here in the Netherlands," explains Alisa, "it's unusual for children to become involved in charitable activities. I hope, through encouraging and supporting our members, to help them change the lives of other kids, and empower them with the knowledge they can make a difference in the world."

Over the past three years, the group has worked to raise awareness of issues affecting children globally through addressing audiences at their school and local churches, at business dinners and community events. Through a variety of creative fundraising strategies, ranging from designing and selling their own Christmas cards to marketing a music CD about children and war, the team has raised a total of €7,000, which has been used to build a classroom in the Masai Mara region in Kenya. The school is providing education to poor indigenous children. Says Frederik, "It was our first goal. People said we couldn't do it, that it was too big and we were too young, but we did."

Focusing on Education

In the early stages of the team's work, members concentrated on learning as much as they could about children's issues. They came to understand, for example, that worldwide, an estimated 250 million children work; nearly a third of whom are under the age of 10. They also became aware that one vital key to eliminating child labor is increasing educational opportunities for children. Right now, 121 million children around the world – most of them girls – are not in school, even though the international community has committed to universal education for all boys and girls by 2015, Alisa explains. Ensuring that more children can attend school means working with entire communities, she says, to increase access to education and provide parents with livelihood options that reduce their dependency upon their children to help support the family. Through participating in Free The Children's "Adopt a Village" campaign, the Rotterdam-Kralingen group seeks to pursue just such a holistic approach to addressing child labor. It helps the whole community, the team members note, so that families don't have to use child labor.

Stijn and the group's mentor, Alisa Kasmir, prepare for a meeting with a potential donor.

Following their initial research phase, the team opted to focus their efforts on providing educational opportunities to children living in the rural village in Kenya, identified by Free The Children as one of its development projects. To learn more about Kenya and its national educational policies, the whole team visited the Kenyan Embassy in The Hague, the capital of the Netherlands. Impressed by the group's efforts, the Kenyan ambassador emphasized that through providing even just a few children with an education, they could influence the future of an entire community.

Fundraising at School and in the Community

While volunteering can be hard and challenging work, the group agrees that it can also be fun. One of the group's first fundraising campaigns involved the sale of a classical music CD, entitled *For Our Children*. When members of the team first approached the principal's office at their school for permission

To learn more about Kenya and its national educational policies, the whole team visited the Kenyan Embassy in The Hague, the capital of the Netherlands.

Team members attend the Rotterdam Marathon to cheer on a participant who supported their fundraising efforts by agreeing to let them approach sponsors for her run.

to sell the CD, they were nervous and a bit scared. "But we practiced what we wanted to say and tried to remember that it was OK to hear 'no,'" recalls Frederik. The principal not only accepted their proposal but also sent a special announcement home to all of the students' parents about the effort. Local shops, too, agreed to sell the CD and donated proceeds to the group's efforts. To date, the group has generated more than €400 from sales of the CD.

During another fundraising exercise, the team asked pupils at the school's annual Easter breakfast to each donate one euro to purchase sports equipment for the school in Kenya. In that one day alone, the group raised more than half the money it needed for the equipment. Leading up to another popular event, the Rotterdam Marathon, team members collaborated with one of the athletes, who supported their fundraising efforts by agreeing to let them approach sponsors for her run.

In what could be a major boost to its fundraising efforts, the group recently met with a vice president of Unilever, one of the world's leading suppliers of consumer goods, at the company's global headquarters in Rotterdam. A parent at their school facilitated the introduction. In typical Dutch style, Stijn and Alisa rode their bikes to the meeting. During the hour and a half–long conversation, Stijn did most of the talking, briefing the executive about Free The Children's work – both globally and locally – and proposing various ways in which the company might get involved. While it's too early now to tell exactly what the outcomes may be, Unilever expressed an interest in helping the group develop a computer game that would educate children about the importance of proper nutrition and exercise as part of the company's efforts to promote healthy lifestyles. The team has already met with a computer design expert, referred to them through one of their parents, about what the game might look like.

"We practiced what we wanted to say and tried to remember that it was OK to hear 'no,'" recalls Frederik.

Growing Yourself through Helping Others

While proud of all they have achieved, members of the team find that volunteering can be demanding, especially when their friends are off playing. Tian Ci admits that at one point he didn't feel like going to meetings and taking notes any more. At the same time, he came across an article in the newspaper describing a young girl in Sierra Leone who was hit by a stray bullet during a battle in her hometown. With the nearest hospital twenty kilometers away, the girl walked for two days to get there. "She was about my age," says Tian Ci. "That really blew me away. I still have the article and am vice president of our chapter now."

Has age ever gotten in the way of the team achieving its goals? "We've learned that if we are very well prepared, know what we're talking about, and are a bit patient, most people come around in the end," says Stijn.

All the members of the group say they have developed greater confidence as a result of their efforts, and are more aware of social issues that affect children around the world. Alisa comments that there have been other noticeable benefits among members, such as learning how to work as a team and listening to and respecting others' ideas.

Perhaps the greatest benefit of all is how the young volunteers feel as a result of their efforts. Says Julius, "I like helping other kids. It just makes me feel good inside, so it must be right." ■

Members work on a project for Koninginnedag (the Queen's birthday).

"When I was twelve, I founded Free The Children with a group of friends. Adults told us that we were 'too young' to make a difference on an issue as complicated as child labor. We were called 'dreamers' when we spoke of starting the world's largest network of children helping children. We were labeled 'idealistic' when we set a goal to raise funds to build one hundred primary schools in developing countries.

Ten years later, Free The Children is the world's largest network of children helping children through education, having impacted the lives of more than a million children in forty-five countries. Our projects include the construction of over four hundred primary schools overseas, and leadership training programs that empower 250,000 students annually in North America. The moral of the story? When someone calls you 'young,' 'idealistic,' and a 'dreamer,' thank them for the compliment."

Craig Kielburger
Founder and Chair Free The Children
Toronto, Canada

ADVICE FROM THE TEAM ON:

Raising Funds to Support Development Projects

- **Partner with an existing organization.** By working as part of Free The Children's global network, the group gained credibility and could direct its donations to trustworthy projects. They also benefited from the use of Free The Children's promotional materials, including stickers, pamphlets, CD-ROMs, and folders.

- **Use your age to your advantage.** Part of the group's appeal is its very youthfulness. During a recent fundraising pitch to a senior executive at a global corporation, the adult mentor of the team said little, letting its 11-year-old president, Stijn, do most of the talking. The company's representative was impressed and took the group's efforts seriously.

- **Don't be afraid to ask for what you want.** At first nervous about approaching their school's principal for permission to sell music CDs, the group marshaled the confidence they needed and were duly rewarded. The principal sent letters out to all of the parents announcing the CD sale and the group's charitable goals.

- **Be creative.** Group members design fundraising campaigns that are fun and that connect to existing events in the community. For example, at Easter they asked students to donate a euro to support children's sports education in Kenya. They also allied with a marathon runner to raise sponsorship funds.

- **Be strategic.** Being strategic means being at the right place at the right time and using your contacts wisely. For example, on New Year's Eve following the December 2004 tsunami in south Asia, the group stood outside a liquor store in the rain to raise money for victims. Their strategy proved a big success.

- **Gain access through networking.** Group members excel at tapping the resources they have close at hand, e.g., their parents and members of the school community. It's really about asking people for help – and knowing some well-connected and talented people, the team notes.

For further information, visit: **www.freethechildren.or**

A Commitment to Grow:
From Local to Global

KAILASH SATYARTHI

CHAIRPERSON
GLOBAL MARCH AGAINST CHILD LABOUR
GLOBAL CAMPAIGN FOR EDUCATION

There are times in each of our lives when, confronted with a social injustice, we are faced with a choice of whether and how to act. Many of you reading this book have already taken action or are seeking the knowledge and tools to do so.

The Global March Against Child Labour has mobilized thousands of people worldwide to protect and promote the rights of children.

For two and a half decades I have worked with and for children and youth who have been deprived of their childhood, freedom, education, health, and, in many cases, their identity and dignity as human beings. I realized early on that morally and ethically I had no choice but to try and undo such injustices. Many people hold the belief that some children are born to work. I couldn't disagree more. It is my conviction that every child is born to enjoy childhood to the fullest, to have access to opportunities to grow, and to have his or her rights honored and protected.

The roots of my activism date back to my first day at school, where I encountered a boy of my age – five or six – sitting on the steps with his father. They were cobblers. As we students entered the school, full of excitement, this boy looked up eagerly, wanting nothing more than to earn a few rupees polishing our shoes. This upset me. I asked my teacher why this child was not attending school. I was told he was poor. I thought, "So what?" But no one could answer me.

Kailash views the elimination of child labor as essential to achieving the Millennium Development Goals established by the international community. "Child labor is the biggest barrier to attaining education for all and poverty alleviation," he emphasizes.

Soon, I gathered my courage and went to the boy's father. I asked him why his son was not in school. The man replied, "My grandfather, father, and myself never went to school. It is the same with my son. We are born to work."

Such answers would never satisfy me. Over time, I found ways to translate my anguish into action. At the end of one school year, a friend and I collected more than two thousand used books, which would have otherwise been thrown away. With the help of teachers, we set up a book bank for children who could not afford them.

Years later, as I began a career in electrical engineering, I realized that my mind and heart could never be fully engaged in such a pursuit while children were enslaved. They were sold and bought like animals – abused, tortured, and forced to work without pay in small factories, mines, brick kilns, and agricultural fields, or inside homes as domestic laborers. I abandoned my career in 1980 and founded an organization to fight child servitude. This was an even greater challenge given that in my country servitude, bondage, and child labor were culturally accepted as normal.

Using the media and the legal and judicial systems, we started by taking direct steps to liberate child slaves. Eventually we realized that this wasn't enough. To get at the root causes of child labor, we would need to build a mass movement. At the heart of this movement would be empowering and encouraging children and youth to assume leadership roles in protecting their own rights.

We organized a series of mass awareness campaigns, including long marches across India and eventually around the world. In 1998, more than seven million people joined the Global March Against Child Labour. The 80,000-kilometer march crossed a hundred countries on five continents and culminated in a major appeal before the International Labour Organization (ILO) General Assembly in Geneva. The Global March is now recognized as the single largest mobilization of people seeking to eliminate child labor worldwide. The March's momentum translated into a worldwide movement: the Global March Against Child Labour (www.globalmarch.org). In all our endeavors, we advocate for the elimination of child labor, illiteracy, and poverty – for none can be eliminated without addressing the other two.

As our work has evolved, we have developed new initiatives, including a child-free-labor labeling system, the building of youth leadership centers in India, and the creation of a national network of child-friendly villages. Each initiative seeks to achieve long-term, systemic changes in the way young people are treated. In the process of developing your own social change projects, you will also be challenged with finding ways to maximize your efforts to achieve the greatest possible impact. As you read this book, my hope is that you will experience a sense of connection and shared purpose with the many young people around the world who are working to promote greater social justice. May each of you contribute to making this world a better place for children and youth. ∎

HA THI LAN ANH

Expressing youth views via radio

VIETNAM

Working in the media gives you the chance to inform people, inspire people, influence people, and connect to people. It means you have to be open minded, and always be willing to get to know others and build contacts. As young broadcasters, we have to speak the voices of young people, and reflect their concerns, needs, and aspirations. But the most important lesson that I've learned is to be brave, to speak out about what you think, and to be open to the different opinions of others.

– Ha Thi Lan Anh

Ha Thi Lan Anh was 14 when she conducted her first interview for radio.

OUR TIME IS NOW

Lan Anh prepares to address the 2004 National Conference of Junior Reporters' Clubs, held in Hanoi.

In addition to an extremely demanding schedule as a hard-working student and young activist, Lan Anh put countless hours into convincing adults of the importance of promoting young voices on the radio.

Eight years ago, Ha Thi Lan Anh, an inquisitive seventh-grader living in Vietnam's capital city of Hanol, listened intently to a group of journalists who were visiting her school. The reporters, who worked for the government-run radio station, came to recruit young people to read stories on the radio. Noting 12-year-old Lan Anh's confident, clear voice, they offered her an internship.

After a few weeks on the job, however, Lan Anh realized that the radio programs failed to adequately reflect the lives or concerns of her peers. "Where are the kids like me who have independent opinions and sometimes get into a little bit of trouble?" she remembers asking at the time. "I was determined to do something new."

Even after writing stories on her own and getting a few of them broadcast, Lan Anh remained deeply frustrated that young people in Vietnam had no way to voice their ideas or their concerns about the world around them. So she and several friends launched Vietnam's first youth journalists' group in 1998. Supported through UNICEF and the government radio station, the Junior Reporters' Club had twenty original members, ages 12 to 14. "We wanted a place to write more freely and to study journalism," Lan Anh explains. "We wanted to be useful and professional."

Expanding Youth Voices in the Media

Every Tuesday and Thursday morning at 7:30, millions of radio listeners across Vietnam tune in to *Children's Aspirations*, a radio program broadcast by the government-run station and produced by the Junior Reporters' Club. More than one thousand young journalists in thirty-nine chapters contribute stories and interviews to the radio broadcasts, as well as to the group's monthly newsletter. Over the past seven years, club members have produced more than seven hundred radio programs, and published articles in print media outlets countrywide.

In love with music, technology, cultures, and writing, Lan Anh is a poised and passionate young woman with an easy laugh and long hair that often falls across her face. Her intensity and steely discipline are evident as she describes the challenges of starting up a youth-led media organization as a young teenager. In addition to an extremely demanding schedule as a hard-working student and young activist, she put countless hours into convincing adults of the importance of promoting young voices on the radio. Particularly in an Asian culture, she explains, young people are taught to follow the rules and respect their elders. But she persevered, knowing that "just because something hasn't been done doesn't mean it can't be done."

Members of the Junior Reporters' Club, which was originally called the Young Journalists' Group, believe that by raising their voices through the media they can help educate and inform the public on issues of concern to youth. Often they pursue stories that adults don't consider "news," such as the plight of orphans, street children, and the disabled. The club members, called Green Bees, also focus on broader themes such as children's rights, pollution, gender equality, and human development. Explaining UNICEF'S initial funding for the program, Misbah Sheikh at UNICEF-Vietnam said, "I feel this organization is incredibly important, not only to serve as an example that youth can be more involved in producing their own media, but in facilitating the creation of other youth-led initiatives such as web pages, hot lines, and other media outlets."

Recognizing the need to train young reporters in basic journalism skills, the club organizes workshops for members to learn how to interview, write, and express themselves. They also learn the technological skills necessary to record interviews and produce radio programs. Adult journalists serve as mentors, sharing their interviewing and writing techniques with the youth.

Experiencing the Challenges of Journalism

Lan Anh was in eighth grade when she conducted her first major radio interview. It was with an American doctor who, as part of Operation Smile, had come to Vietnam to treat young children with facial deformities. "He was very busy, and it was difficult to pin him down for an interview," she admits. "My friends and I ran around the hospital, trying to find him." When she finally located the doctor, he appeared awestruck that his interviewer was so young and had waited so long. For Lan Anh, it was worth the effort. "During the interview, this doctor was teaching me and I was learning so much; about him, about the children, about myself."

Lan Anh still remembers her most difficult interview – with a group of street children. Unsure of whether they would talk with her, Lan Anh first approached them at a community center where they received food and services. "They looked at me like I was an alien," she recalls. At first Lan Anh tried to interview them on tape, but they did not want her to continue. So she decided to give them the tape recorder, and then they became more interested in her and what she was doing. "I needed them to trust me," she explains. The street children finally agreed to be interviewed, and when they heard themselves on the radio, they were excited. "Some of them wrote to me after that," Lan Anh says, smiling.

Club reporters, called Green Bees, focus their stories on such subjects as children's rights, pollution, and the plight of street children and the disabled.

In explaining why she believes radio is such a powerful communications tool, Lan Anh points out that most Vietnamese citizens don't own a television, having far greater access to radio. Also, many young people living in rural areas work in the fields in the morning. They can listen to radio programs like *Children's Aspirations* over an

In 2004, club members were introduced to a new form of creative expression: documentary filmmaking.

Lan Anh was one of twelve delegates selected from Vietnam to attend the United Nations General Assembly's Special Session on Children held in New York City in May 2002.

outside loudspeaker while they work. Lan Anh also believes that when young people watch TV, they focus on whether the speaker is handsome or beautiful, but they don't listen to what is being said. "The radio is more lively, and people are more apt to pay attention to your story and your message," she asserts.

Developing Leadership Skills

While training a younger generation of journalists is a key goal for the Junior Reporters' Club, the program also provides a rare opportunity to nurture a sense of civic responsibility among its members. Through reporting on local issues, club reporters engage with community members and develop knowledge around urgent social concerns. Past stories have focused on the pollution of Hanoi's rivers, the importance of nurturing an environmental ethic within schools, and ways in which youth can volunteer. For Lan Anh and her colleagues, membership in the club is a way to spur their peers to be part of the solution. "That's why we want to be more than youth journalists," she comments. "We see ourselves as youth activists and youth innovators."

To further inject young people's voices in the decision-making process, the Junior Reporters' Club began to organize local and national forums that brought youth together

with government leaders, social workers, and community leaders around the country. They also organized the first meeting between youth and top government officials, including the president of Vietnam and the prime minister. The result: Lan Anh and her group were invited to participate and comment on the country's national action plan for children over the next decade.

Lan Anh was one of twelve delegates selected from Vietnam to attend the United Nations General Assembly's Special Session on Children held in New York City in May 2002, where she delivered a message to UN Secretary-General Kofi Annan. "We stressed children's rights, youth participation, and youth empowerment," says Lan Anh. "At the time, these were new issues in Vietnam for adults and for youth – but [they] are too important not to be addressed."

Transferring Ownership and Moving On

Today, at 21, Lan Anh is a second-year, full-scholarship student at Trent University in Ontario, Canada, with a dual major in international political economy and development studies. However, she remains closely connected to the Junior Reporters' Club, serving as a senior advisor and part-time fundraiser for the organization. She describes the club's ongoing progress with pride. In early 2005, for example, Plan International, a U.S.-based nonprofit organization, adopted its model of training young journalists and is now in the process of establishing similar groups in cities across the country. The club is also expanding its work into other forms of media, including documentary films.

Lan Anh is deeply involved in community issues in her new home, working alongside her Canadian friends and fellow students to have a positive impact on people's lives. In her "free time," she regularly volunteers for a mentoring program that matches college students with mentally disabled youth in Canada.

The transition to her new life has been both exciting and difficult. "I think it's a hard decision to leave a project that you created and move on with your life and new experiences," she says. Yet she's pleased that her former colleagues in the Junior Reporters' Club have become leaders in their communities, in addition to mentoring new reporters. Lan Anh's experience championing young people's right to have a voice remains a powerful force in her life today. "It has been a source of inspiration for me to continue my activism and passion to work for people and social justice." ∎

Over the past seven years, the Junior Reporters' Club has produced more than seven hundred radio programs and has published articles in print media countrywide.

"The make-believe of radio is what drew me to it as a young girl. My favorite program was called Let's Pretend. *All those years ago, before the age of television, radio told me stories [and] transported me to new worlds, ideas, encounters. For more than thirty years now, at the microphones of National Public Radio, I've been telling real stories on the air, and learning how powerful the real and the imagined can be in this marvelous medium where the pictures are always better, because we make them in our mind's eye. I'm so moved by young Lan Anh in Vietnam, who is committed to using radio to improve and change the world in which she lives. The voices of young people must be heard throughout the world. How marvelous that Lan Anh has made that happen in her own country – to the benefit of millions of listeners."*

Susan Stamberg
Special Correspondent National Public Radio
Washington, D.C., United States

ADVICE FROM LAN ANH ON:

Creating a Youth-Led Media Initiative

- **Work on your skills; enthusiasm is not enough.** A top priority of the Junior Reporters' Club is to organize workshops to improve members' writing and interviewing skills. To be successful, Lan Anh says, "Young people have to have both youthful creativity and professional skills. Educate yourself. Read newspapers, improve your writing skills, talk to journalists you know. Then it will be harder for people to say no to you."

- **Create an effective management structure.** To develop a network of journalists, you must build a strong organizing structure. In the beginning, the Junior Reporters' Club had to coordinate a network of three hundred youth journalists working out of eight regional offices all over the country. As a result, they needed to create an effective and strong management structure at the local level. By electing a board of managers at each office, which worked directly with the organization's headquarters in Hanoi, the club was able to keep in touch with local reporters while coordinating the placement of their interviews at a central location.

- **Plan for the future.** In order to ensure continuation of the program, the Junior Reporters' Club members developed a strategy based on mentorship and peer training, with senior journalists in the group training the younger ones. As a result, new leaders emerge and run the organization when the "seniors" leave.

- **Recognize that intergenerational learning is important, but challenging.** From the beginning, Lan Anh tapped into the experience and support of adult professionals in the media field, who often served as mentors to the young journalists. Yet Lan Anh cautions that adults often don't take young people seriously, especially in an Asian culture where children are supposed to obey adults, and not break the rules.

- **Partner with an existing broadcast outlet.** While Lan Anh and her corps of young journalists had enthusiasm and creativity, they did not have the resources or infrastructure to launch their own radio program. The sponsorship of the state-run radio station was vital, providing the young reporters with technical assistance, radios, tapes, and the use of the station itself to broadcast the Club's reports.

JOHN CHUKWUDI BAKO

Harnessing the power of media to combat HIV/AIDS

NIGERIA

I was inspired to establish this initiative after I heard the heartbreaking story of a woman who was infected by HIV by her husband, who eventually abandoned her and her newborn baby. As I heard this terrible story over the radio, I began to imagine the pain, stigma, and discrimination this woman was subjected to simply because she was HIV positive. I could not understand why her husband and family members abandoned her at such a critical stage in her life, at a time when she needed them most. One word came to my mind: ignorance.

– John Chukwudi Bako

Action E3 on AIDS Nigeria focuses on the three E's: education, enlightenment, and eradication.

At 22, John Chukwudi Bako was halfway through his government-mandated community service in the state of Borno in northeast Nigeria when he took steps to combat the spread of HIV/AIDS. Through his work as a secondary school teacher, John witnessed firsthand young people's lack of education and awareness about the disease. The situation was echoed in the wider community. It seemed like every week John would hear another devastating story of someone who had been infected by HIV/AIDS, or someone who lied to a spouse or relative about contracting the disease. The epidemic fueled an environment of distrust, disloyalty, and misinformation that seriously impeded any concerted effort to control it.

"I realized people needed to be properly reoriented," says John. "I wanted to debunk and correct all the misleading perceptions most Nigerians had about HIV/AIDS."

In 2001, John founded Action E3 on AIDS Nigeria, a nongovernmental organization that works to educate the public about the nature, effects, treatment, and prevention of HIV/AIDS. The organization's efforts focus on the three E's: education, enlightenment, and eradication. John's own understanding of the disease was reinforced through a UNICEF-sponsored HIV/AIDS training course that qualified him to serve as a master trainer. In the early days of Action E3's work,

John facilitates a training program in Biu in northeast Nigeria.

UNICEF, along with the Society for Family Health and the Catholic Diocese of Maiduguri, provided technical assistance. Financial support came from the National Youth Service Corps, the Borno State Primary Education Board, and the United Bank for Africa Biu.

"We do all of this because we believe information is power," John explains.

Over the past four years, Action E3 on AIDS Nigeria has employed a variety of creative strategies to communicate HIV/AIDS messages in an accessible way – on the radio, via the Internet, and through songs, dramatic performances, and folktales. To reach as many people as possible, Action E3 targets its campaigns to achieve a widespread impact; for example, training students to serve as peer educators in schools, approaching commuters on buses, and most recently, through training football (soccer) captains to convey vital health information to their teammates. Its strategy is rooted in the concept of "edutainment," whereby important messages are embedded in popular forms of entertainment. "We do all of this because we believe information is power," John explains, "and that when people are better informed, they know what to do."

To date, Action E3 has reached more than twenty thousand students in schools and communities in some of the poor rural and urban areas of the country where information on HIV/AIDS is limited. In addition, more than a million commuters have received vital health information through the organization's Mobile Behavior Change Communication (MBCC), carried out on buses. Other pilot projects and seminars have been held in businesses, police stations, churches, and army barracks, as well as among factory workers and prisoners.

Tailoring Your Message to Your Audience

According to official estimates, one in twenty Nigerians is infected with HIV/AIDS, and the country currently reports the highest number of HIV/AIDS cases in West Africa. Since 1986, when the disease was first discovered in Nigeria, as many as 1.5 million of the nation's citizens have died. This year alone, the disease will claim roughly forty thousand Nigerian children and leave another 1.5 million orphaned.

For John, and Action E3's full- and part-time staff of twelve, there is no more urgent issue facing the country. With AIDS striking older youth and adults in the prime of their productive years, the disease has serious implications for the country's social, economic, and political future. For health communicators, the challenge remains when and where to reach their target audience and how to craft messages that will capture people's attention and interest.

One of Action E3's most successful and far-reaching HIV/AIDS awareness campaigns is being carried out on the nation's bus system. Says John, "Most people go to work very early. We reach them before they get to the office, while their minds are less consumed and they don't have much to do." Trained volunteers interact with passengers, providing them with educational flyers and engaging them in conversation about the issue.

Reflecting the fact that 60 percent of the nation's population is under the age of 24, much of Action E3's work focuses on young people – either as recipients of services or valuable allies in delivering those services. To date, the organization has trained more than fifty peer educators who lead HIV/AIDS prevention campaigns in schools around the country.

Starting in 2004, Action E3 began collaborating with *Watchdog Nigeria*, a morning radio show, to deliver a daily fifteen-minute program. During the segment, an HIV/AIDS expert responds to questions posed by the show's presenter. Listeners, some of them living with the disease, call in to share their own experiences and seek advice. Surveys of audience members found that 75 percent had increased their knowledge and understanding of HIV/AIDS. Similarly, in 2005, Action E3 initiated an email behavior change campaign through which it sends emails containing reproductive health messages to young people included within its growing database.

In a lecture before members of the Federal Road Safety Corps, John uses a poster created by UNICEF as a teaching aid.

Combining HIV/AIDS Education with Sports

John facilitates a training program at a high school.

Action E3's latest strategy involves strengthening the leadership skills of youth who run HIV/AIDS initiatives, so that they, in turn, can train the captains of local football teams. "In Nigeria, football is like a religion," says John. "We have young people playing football on the streets. Everyplace that is available, people want to play."

Action E3 is carrying out the training in collaboration with Leadership Effectiveness Accountability & Professionalism (LEAP) Africa, a national NGO. Funding for the training is being provided by Nokia, with additional technical support coming from the Society for Family Health and the Lagos State AIDS Control Agency. Over a five-week period, participants learn core leadership skills, such as project planning, interpersonal communication, responsibility, self-confidence, and time management. They also learn techniques for working with young leaders in a sports context, so that they are best able to connect with the football captains. Following the training, each participant is asked to identify and share what he or she has learned with ten or more football captains. Through equipping local sports figures with the ability to deliver HIV/AIDS education to their teammates, Action E3 hopes to promote their role as agents of positive social change.

"They (the football captains) go back to their clubs and share their experience with people," John explains. "They're going to discuss it with their families. They're going to expand the knowledge they've gained by sharing it with others."

Maintaining a Positive Attitude

Over the past few years, experts estimate that the prevalence of HIV/AIDS has actually fallen – if only slightly – in Nigeria. While John acknowledges that the current situation is still extremely grave, he remains hopeful for the future, particularly in light of the growing commitment of young people to fighting the disease. "With awareness campaigns against the disease, which are currently going on in the country, people are becoming better educated than they were a few years ago," he says. "Youth want to be involved as well, having realized that they are more vulnerable to HIV. Many of them want to make a contribution, especially if they can find platforms to do so." Through its leadership training and peer education activities, this is precisely what Action E3 seeks to achieve.

"People are becoming better educated than they were a few years ago," says John.

A devout Christian, John attributes his own strength as a leader to his faith in God, hard work, and his passionate commitment to eliminating the spread of the disease. Although he deals with a life-or-death issue each day, he strives to focus on the positive. Friends describe John as upbeat, energetic, and innovative when it comes to developing creative solutions to complex social problems. He also mirrors the behaviors he advocates. Deeply disturbed by the stigma and discrimination related to the disease, John talks, shares meals, and interacts regularly with those who have been infected.

Asked if his life has changed as a result of his work, John responds affirmatively. While he once dreamed of working in an embassy or joining the Nigerian Foreign Service, he is now dedicated to improving public health education and strengthening youth leadership in the country. Today, he can't imagine doing anything different than his present job: "What I think of and dream of is how to curb the spread of HIV in my community, which threatens to tear apart the social fabric of Nigeria." ■

Action E3 on AIDS Nigeria pursues a variety of creative strategies to communicate health messages to specific audiences, such as commuters traveling on the nation's bus system.

"John Chukwudi Bako's passion for change and urgent sense of mission influence everything that he does."

Ndidi Okonkwo Nwuneli
Founder and CEO LEAP Africa
Lagos, Nigeria

"To meet the challenges of our time, humanity must develop a greater sense of responsibility. Each of us must learn to work not just for our self, our family, or our nation, but also for the benefit of mankind."

His Holiness the Dalai Lama
Spiritual Leader of the People of Tibet
Nobel Peace Prize Laureate
Dharamsala, India

ADVICE FROM JOHN ON:

Communicating Important Health Messages

- **Carefully identify those audiences you wish to reach and develop appropriate messages.** Action E3 pursues different approaches depending on whether it seeks to capture the attention of high school students or prison inmates; factory workers or military personnel. Knowing whom you want to reach, what their interests are, and when and how to best approach them are critical to making sure your message gets through.

- **Determine which medium(s) will be best suited for reaching your target audience.** Action E3 on AIDS Nigeria recognized that it could reach thousands of people through a regularly scheduled radio call-in show. Handing out educational leaflets on buses proved to be an excellent way of reaching morning commuters, and sending health-related emails to young people maximized the use of a youth-friendly technology.

- **Network and collaborate with established organizations.** Action E3's work was strengthened through the technical assistance it received from UNICEF, various government agencies, and local NGOs. Affiliations with such organizations can add legitimacy to your work and enable you to achieve greater impact through sharing resources and expertise.

- **Conduct surveys to determine your audience's level of knowledge.** Action E3 on AIDS surveyed students to determine their current knowledge concerning HIV/AIDS transmission and their behavior patterns.

- **Identify existing resources.** Many excellent materials are available for conducting educational outreach around important health issues. Most recently, Action E3 has reinforced its training activities through the use of an educational film, *Positive Voices – Positive Choices*, produced by the Johns Hopkins Center for Communication Programs in the United States.

- **Educate and train others to carry out your organization's mission.** Over time, Action E3 has trained more than fifty peer educators who work in schools to inform their peers about HIV/AIDS transmission and the preventive measures they can take.

ANDRÉS BEIBE & AGUSTÍN FRIZZERA

Teaching students about their role in a democracy

ARGENTINA

We used to listen to our friends say that "every Argentine politician should leave office," "all of them are corrupt," "our country has no exit but the airport," and so on. Through Ágora, we developed a tool that allows us to educate young people who will soon be voting about their political system. We knew we had to approach them in a dynamic way. It couldn't be a book, a speech, or a poster. They had to reach conclusions by themselves. That's why we designed a game, a role-playing exercise, through which each student can develop their understanding of the political and social situation in Argentina.

– Andrés Beibe

Ágora team members participate in a media training session.

We teach students how to participate in building a strong democracy. It wasn't easy at first. At the beginning, most of the public schools shut their doors to us. But once we tested and proved it could work, they accepted us. . . . Not only have the students changed, but I've changed. I've seen people I never thought I'd see before. I've gone to places so poor; yet so rich. I'm more empathetic and communicate better. We're not about prescribing how to act, but getting students to think and take action around issues they care about.

– Agustín Frizzera

Ágora participants engage in a role-playing exercise.

On the second floor of the Colegio Botánico, a secondary school in the Argentine capital of Buenos Aires, more than thirty high school students dart back and forth between tables stretched along a hall. Each is involved in intense negotiations over the future of a fictional nation. The role-playing game they undertake is both fun and serious business. Divided into special-interest groups – including the army, teachers' union, church, industrial federation, and rural farmers' association – they lobby members of Parliament about the importance of funding their constituents' needs. At the end of the afternoon, the president of this mock country will announce how the nation's annual budget will be spent. As with most intense political debates, there will be winners and losers.

"They (the students) come to appreciate that the democratic process is an important thing and that the opinions of minority groups really matter," says Agustín.

Orchestrating this chaotic scene is Agustín Frizzera, the 25-year-old co-founder of Ágora: Educating for Democracy, a program that educates students, ages 16 to 18, about democracy and responsibilities as citizens.

At the end of the game, the students talk and reflect on what happened. Those that didn't receive the funding they requested voice their frustration. In the process, they learn that politics often involves compromise and consider how they might articulate their needs more effectively in the future. Says Agustín, "Through the process, they come to appreciate that the democratic process is an important thing and that the opinions of minority groups really matter."

The game is only part of the story. Two weeks prior to the role-playing exercise, the students studied and discussed the contents of a booklet they received describing Argentina's political system, how the national budget is created, and how laws are passed. Later, after playing the simulation game, members of the group will learn how to design and carry out volunteer projects, such as neighborhood cleanups, in their communities. Through this three-stage approach, Ágora works to prepare the emerging generation of Argentine voters to participate actively in the political process.

Ágora is the brainchild of Agustín and his best friend, Andrés Beibe. The two met while playing football against one another at the age of 12. Over the years, their friendship grew, as did their concern for the future of their country. It was hardly surprising when, a decade after their first encounter on a football field, the two joined forces in battling a growing problem in Argentina: a pervasive lack of faith among the nation's citizens in their political system.

Agustín and Andrés created Ágora in 2001 during one of the worst economic and political crises in Argentina's history. A prolonged recession, high unemployment, and a national banking crisis had prompted widespread food riots and demonstrations. During elections that year, Argentinians rejected all politicians – thrusting empty envelopes and pieces of paper with insults into ballot boxes. What became known as a *vota bronca*, or anger vote, signaled people's loss of faith in the democratic process.

"Argentinians were tired of how politicians were running their country," recalls Andrés. "At the same time, they lacked understanding of the importance of building channels of active civic participation." Who better to devise a solution than two smart, energetic university students?

The word *Ágora* has its roots in ancient Greece, where it referred to a public square at which people gathered to discuss important political issues. For Andrés and Agustín, the term symbolizes their goal to stimulate young people's interest and involvement in the political process. Ágora does so through teaching high school students how government works, engaging them in lively debates about urgent issues in their country, and providing them with opportunities to serve the greater community.

Its young founders designed Ágora as an antidote for apathy. By focusing their efforts on high school seniors, not yet tied to a political party, Andrés and Agustín hoped to usher in a new era of active citizen participation. "Ágora is essential to helping young citizens understand how decisions are made at the government level and to be fully aware of the advantages and limitations of the democratic system in Argentina," says Andrés.

Since the program started, it has reached more than 2,800 students in Buenos Aires and three other Argentine cities. Building on its track record, Ágora is now being expanded to Uruguay, with Paraguay soon to follow.

Increasingly, the program is capturing the attention of local nongovernmental organizations (NGOs), national and international donors, and the media. "I'm a big fan of Ágora," says Belén Maggi, program administrator of Proyecto Iniciativa Popular, an Argentine NGO that works to improve people's understanding of existing laws while advocating policies that allow for greater citizen participation. Maggi commends Agustín and Andrés' efforts to advocate for the positive roles that young people can play in society. "They treat students as future voters and show them their rights and responsibilities," he says. "Young people here are not always viewed as mature individuals that have the possibility of making our country a better one."

Ágora co-founder Agustín Frizzera.

Working Together as Partners

When asked about the factors that contributed to their success, Andrés and Agustín say it all came down to hard work, perseverance, and the ability to work well together. While they share similar goals, they admit they're different in other ways. Yet it's those very differences that contributed to making them a good team.

A Commitment to Grow: **From Local to Global**

Ágora team members from Argentina and Paraguay meet in Buenos Aires.

At the time they started Ágora, Agustín – tall, lean, and practical – was completing a major in sociology, and Andrés – curly-headed with a spontaneous, warm smile – was finishing up his university studies in political science. Agustín found his strengths in planning and carrying out the program's activities. He soon discovered that he preferred interacting with students to impressing donors. "With the kids, I could be myself," he says. "I didn't have to show off."

Andrés was naturally predisposed to management and fundraising. The Ágora concept was initially his idea, but it was Agustín who urged him to take action, providing some of the initial seed funding to get the program off the ground. "In order to have vision, I leaned on him," says Andrés of his relationship with Agustín. Their approach to life can also be different. While Andrés plans his life carefully and stays focused on objectives, Agustín admits he prefers to "build his road by walking."

Andrés and Agustín knew that they needed adult allies to help achieve their goals.

Critical to their work together has been the importance of trust and open communication. "We talked about everything that bothered us and swore at each other a lot," says Andrés. "We could be honest without hurting each other's feelings."

Also important was maintaining accountability. Although there were times when the two had to forgo work to study, both always fulfilled their responsibilities.

According to Iniciativa Popular's Maggi, the personalities of the duo have had as much as anything to do with their success. "They have charisma and they work hard," says Maggi, "Young people see them as a good example, but also as cool guys."

Building a Team

Equally important was building the rest of their team. From a core group of four, Ágora's staffing needs quickly grew, and before they knew it, Andrés and Agustín were managing sixteen volunteers. Each volunteer committed to working four hours every week in fulfilling a variety of responsibilities, from scheduling school visits to researching funding opportunities. Agustín explains that the real challenge behind having a successful volunteer effort is getting the work done while maintaining what he calls the "heart commitment" of the volunteers. "When carrying out day-to-day activities, you don't always feel the mysticism," he adds.

In addition to building a core group of committed staff and volunteers, Andrés and Agustín knew that they needed adult allies to help achieve their goals. Toward that end, they formed a Consultative

Committee to help guide their efforts and open doors to potential funders. Today, the seven-member committee includes the vice-chairman of Gallup Argentina, a public opinion research firm; two university professors; two prominent business owners; and the leader of a nonprofit public policy development organization. The committee has been instrumental in helping to establish priorities, plan for growth, and access valuable networks.

With the proper team in place, and basic funding secured from a local businessman, Agustín and Andrés launched their initial activities from a small, donated office. Over time, Ágora slowly refined its approach and expanded its reach, while taking care to measure results. According to a 2003 survey, 73 percent of participants reported that Ágora had changed their perception of politics, with 99 percent recommending that the program be offered in other schools.

Having built its track record over time, Ágora now receives funding from diverse sources, including universities, foundations, and corporations such as Unilever, Total Austral, and Nestlé Argentina. It has also won the endorsement of the Ministry of Education, which has dubbed it a "Program of National Interest."

As it has evolved, Ágora has had to adjust to leader-ship changes, with Andrés transitioning out of the organization to embark on a career in the private sector and Agustín opting to pursue a master's degree. Far from abandoning their social enterprise, both still serve as advisors as Ágora grows.

Ágora's expansion to neighboring Uruguay is proof of its adaptability and appeal. There, it is being led by Fabrizio Scrollini, a recent law school graduate who met Andrés and Agustín at a conference and got excited about what they were doing. The model has proven easily adaptable to the Uruguayan context, thanks in part to similarities in the two nations' political structures. Following the lead set by the program's founders, Fabrizio started out by engaging his friends as key partners in carrying out the program, and in 2005 Ágora-Uruguay expects to reach students in eight schools. With plans underway to launch the program in Paraguay also, the ancient Greek tradition of lively political debate is spreading quickly through Latin American high schools.

Fabrizio Scrollini liked the idea of Ágora so much that he's taken the program to Uruguay.

"The IDB has long promoted the active participation of Latin American and Caribbean youth in the development process, seeking to engage them as agents of change at the community, national, and international levels. The fruits of the Bank's efforts demonstrate the importance of fostering youth leadership and the participation of young people in the life of their societies and the world at large."

Enrique V. Iglesias
Former President Inter-American Development Bank
Washington, D.C., United States

ADVICE FROM ANDRÉS & AGUSTÍN ON:

Building Your Team

· **Find people you can trust, who know what they're doing, and who exhibit passion for your cause.** Be sure their life goals are in alignment with your mission. "Try to understand what others want for themselves and for the organization," says Andrés. Follow your instincts in selecting them.

· **Take time to educate staff and volunteers about your organization's vision and goals.** Provide them with a thorough orientation on your organization's work. Consider preparing an operational manual so that a detailed record exists in the event of staff turnover.

· **Communicate well.** Be clear about goals and expectations; provide constructive feedback.

· **Set a good example.** Says Agustín, "Volunteers saw us working all the time."

Developing an Advisory Board

· **Identify key contacts among your friends and family.** Invest time also in expanding your network and identifying people who can help fill gaps in those areas of expertise you need.

· **Be clear with prospective board members about what their responsibilities will be.** Put your expectations (e.g., regular attendance at meetings, monetary donations) in writing.

· **Find out what board members' interests are.** Look for synergies between their interests and your project's goals.

· **Select advisors who have diverse areas of expertise.** Ágora's Consultative Committee includes prominent individuals from the nonprofit, business, and academic communities.

· **Consider dividing the team into task groups that have responsibility for achieving specific goals.** Two of Ágora's committee members have been instrumental in opening doors with international donors.

For further information, visit: **www.interrupcion.ne**

JYOTI MOHAPATRA

Promoting the rights of women and girls

INDIA

I believe that change comes from the power of youth. Youth are in the forefront, because they ask questions that no one else dares to ask. . . . You don't need to leave your community to solve problems. Everyplace you stand, there are enough problems and needs to be addressed. So don't look someplace else. The challenge is right in front of you: your family, your community, on your street.

– Jyoti Mohapatra

Today, more than three hundred Meena Clubs have been established, with a focus on empowering women and girls.

Women and girls in India face enormous social and economic obstacles to realizing their potential. Roughly 40 percent of the nation's 200 million children do not attend school, and most of them are girls.

"My growing up was no different from other girls and women, unprotected and suppressed," recalls Jyoti of her childhood.

On a sunny afternoon in the coastal Indian village of Kendrapara (five hundred kilometers south of Calcutta), Jyotirmayee "Jyoti" Mohapatra and a group of young women and girls are seated on the porch of a small house, engaged in a lively discussion. Their conversation centers on the dowry system, an illegal yet common marriage custom in India whereby a bride's family makes payments in cash or property to the bridegroom's family. One member of the group brings up the extreme practice of "bride burning" – when brides are burned to death because their dowries are considered insufficient. This is an outlawed practice, but one that still takes place in some rural Indian communities. Other members of the group express their concerns over the growing problem of child abuse in the village, and the fact that there are no nearby secondary schools, so girls have to walk long distances, putting them at risk.

At the end of the meeting, the participants determine together what can be done to address some of these challenges and then divide themselves into committees responsible for carrying out their assignments. The fact that these women are meeting together is itself unusual given India's male-dominated society, where most women and girls remain isolated and disenfranchised, particularly in the rural areas. That they are part of a growing movement in India of women's empowerment groups is considered by many to be revolutionary.

Empowering Girls and Women

Ensuring that girls and women find their voices – and become leaders and problem solvers in their communities – is at the heart of a growing network of girls' groups across India called Meena Clubs. Jyoti, along with a small group of girls, helped Nature's Club (a local nongovernmental organization) to first launch the Meena Club concept in 1999. Today, more than three hundred Meena Clubs operate in the state of Orissa on the east coast of India, where Jyoti grew up.

Giving voice to this vulnerable segment of society is a particularly urgent and challenging mission in India. While progress is being made, women and girls face enormous barriers to realizing their full rights and potential. The state of girls' education – while improving – remains a particularly significant roadblock. Roughly 40 percent of the nation's 200 million children and youth do not attend school, most of them girls. Not even one in five girls finishes secondary school, and nearly 40 percent of 15- to 19-year-olds are teenage mothers. Child labor is also a significant problem in India, with forty-four million children in that country reportedly working.

Jyoti's drive to empower women and girls is deeply rooted in her own life experience. "My growing up was no different from other girls and women, unprotected and suppressed," recalls Jyoti of her childhood in Kendrapara. "Children were invisible and women were not treated properly." Most of her peers didn't finish school, and her own parents, afraid for her safety, initially barred her from going to college. While she eventually went to university and received her master's degree, she explains, "I grew up being very aware of how women and girls were suppressed in our society, and the obstacles they had to overcome."

Mobilizing an Often-Ignored Segment of Society

At the age of 19, while completing her degree, Jyoti returned to her village to explore ways of improving the conditions and lives of girls and women. Along with a few friends, she knocked on the doors of every house in the village to see if the women and girls in the families wanted to gather for an informal meeting. Only five girls showed up the first day, but each welcomed the chance to talk openly about her life. By the time Jyoti held the second gathering, more than sixty young women were ready to attend.

In 1999, as Jyoti and her friends began to organize these informal girls' groups, a popular series of animated films developed by UNICEF was being distributed widely across south Asia. The film series told the story of Meena, a young girl who quickly became a beloved role model and powerful symbol of the movement to end discrimination against women and girls. The films, shown by Nature's Club in Jyoti's village, were used as a way to initiate discussions among young viewers, who would meet afterward to talk about the issues raised in the series. The stories of Meena, this courageous new heroine, spread across the region, and the growing network of girls' groups initiated by Jyoti and others became known as the Meena Clubs. "Girls want to do something more, want to expand their leadership roles," Jyoti says. "The film helped spark this idea."

Club members soon began to participate in cultural programs and local festivals. They also started tackling tough social and economic challenges, including child labor and infant and maternal mortality. Participants often divided themselves into committees and took responsibility for certain aspects of the community, such as sanitation, education, health, and emergency relief. In 1999, not long after the clubs began to take shape, a devastating cyclone swept across coastal areas of Orissa. "Meena girls," as they became known, joined hands with rescue teams and helped the victims by distributing relief materials and improving community hygiene and public health.

Developing Problem Solvers

For a year, Meena Club members in one village conducted a monthly health survey of family members. Each family answered questions such as whether they cut their nails, took regular baths, used the latrine, and cleaned up the yard. They were also asked about their health, and whether they had suffered from the flu.

At the age of 19, Jyoti returned to her village to explore ways of improving the conditions and lives of girls and women.

Women and girls who belong to Meena Clubs benefit from having a safe place to talk about issues important to their lives.

Simply asking the questions raised people's awareness about how to lead healthier lives, says Jyoti. "This kind of activity sensitizes people to the issues, but the point here is not to come up with the solution," she explains. "You can't dictate to people how to change; they need to learn themselves, so that they own the solution." At the end of the year, Meena Club members revealed the results of the health survey at a community meeting and calculated how much money the village could have saved if proper health systems and healthy habits were established. "The girls informed the villagers that they could have saved thirty thousand rupees – enough to pay for a teacher for their school," Jyoti recalls proudly.

Local government leaders express increasing enthusiasm about the role Meena Clubs play in improving social and economic conditions in the region. Says the head of district administration in Kendrapara, "The Meena Groups have helped us in achieving results, in the social service sector, health, nutrition, family welfare, and primary education. . . . We would like to extend this kind of experiment as a government-sponsored project for community mobilization."

In explaining the growing movement around women's and girls' empowerment, Jyoti admits it hasn't been easy. "We realized that problems cannot be resolved with aggression,

that it helps if we are soft spoken and non-threatening," she comments.

UNICEF, through Nature's Club, supported the Meena Club movement for the first three years. Although funds have been raised from other sources since then, the clubs continue to need additional funding to acquire computers, expand meeting spaces, and support training programs around child rights and other issues. While fundraising is now a serious concern, Jyoti has big plans for the clubs' future. "Our ultimate goal is to create a child-friendly society," says Jyoti, her thin frame fairly bursting with energy and purpose.

Changing Values and Attitudes

Today, more than eleven thousand Meena girls living in Orissa are volunteering in a wide range of activities aimed at improving life in their communities. The clubs offer a safe place for girls and women to talk more freely about difficult social and personal issues. "Part of change is being able to have honest talk," Jyoti says, underscoring the need for ongoing conversations about sexual abuse, the dowry system, and other "taboo" subjects often ignored by the broader community. But talking is just the beginning.

The clubs also offer participants a chance to become leaders themselves. The nontraditional structure of the Meena Clubs encourages that kind of personal growth. The clubs reject any sense of

According to local government officials, members of the Meena Clubs have helped to improve the living conditions in their communities – in areas such as health, nutrition, and education.

While fundraising is now a serious concern, Jyoti has big plans for the clubs' future.

hierarchy. Members do not elect a president, vice president, or treasurer, and formal membership is not required. Everyone is invited to join. "I don't want there to be elected leaders," says Jyoti. "A 10-year-old can also be a mentor, and can have equal standing within the group. This is what builds leaders and confidence."

Beyond developing leaders, the Meena Clubs are helping to shift public opinion about the role of women and girls in society. For instance, Jyoti explains, "We've found that when girls join a Meena Club, it begins to change the attitude of boys. They know that these girls are intelligent and questioning people, and boys begin to see them as 'cool.'" As a result, she says, some boys are reconsidering the tradition of dowries, because they realize that the girls who join the Meena Clubs may not want to be part of that system.

In some villages, changes are slowly being made in the way decisions are reached. For example, Meena Club members in several communities bring together different groups – such as parents and local government representatives – to discuss issues such as a lack of books in school or the inadequate supply of teachers. Says Jyoti, "Club members try to persuade their elders that young people need to prepare for the task of taking care of society, and that the elders need to help them learn by giving them responsibilities and ensuring they are part of the decision-making process." Jyoti reports that women in a number of villages are now allowed to join the village councils.

On occasion, club members use more direct tactics to protect the rights of women and girls. In one instance, when an elderly man raped a young woman, villagers fined him one hundred rupees for the misconduct. Members of the local Meena Club gathered at the village council and refused to leave until the man was arrested by the police and punished.

"Meena is a concept about balancing a society, where men and women are equal," Jyoti explains. "I want to take this idea all over India, and all over the world." When asked about her personal plans for the future, she replies with a dazzling smile: "I want to be prime minister one day." ∎

Every member of a Meena Club is considered an equal, and there are no elected officials. This informal structure, according to Jyoti, encourages all members, even the youngest ones, to think of themselves as leaders.

"'Women hold up half the sky.' These words of a well-known Chinese proverb underscore the vital role women can – and must – play in shaping our world. At Vital Voices, we celebrate and support women who are emerging as peacemakers, political and economic leaders, and human rights advocates. Through her courageous and inspiring work in India, Jyoti is empowering thousands of women and girls to be agents of change in their communities, by ensuring they have the skills and confidence to effectively raise their voices."

Melanne Verveer
Chairman of the Board Vital Voices
Washington, D.C., United States

ADVICE FROM JYOTI ON:

Building a Leadership Development Network

- **Keep it inclusive.** The Meena Clubs pursue a simple mission to empower girls and women to become leaders and be actively involved in issues that they care about. While most members are girls, everyone in the community is invited to join. This openness reflects the belief that each individual is responsible for improving society, and no one should be left out. Says Jyoti, "We believe that unity is our strength, so we want to involve the entire community."

- **Don't dictate the solution.** Meena Club members believe that to improve conditions or to change opinions, people need to discover the answers by themselves. Says Jyoti, "The point is not to come up with a solution. You can't dictate to people how to change. They need to learn themselves, so that they own the solution."

- **Make it nonhierarchical.** According to Jyoti, one of the most effective ways to develop young leaders is to create nonhierarchical organizations. The Meena Clubs have no elected leaders and are not registered with the government. The clubs comprise an informal network, loosely tied together through their commitment to empowering women and girls. This approach is based on the philosophy that when everyone has an equal voice and equal value, then particularly the younger members are more likely to feel confident and emerge as leaders. At the heart of Jyoti's theory on leadership is the belief that: "A 10-year-old can be a mentor, and can have equal standing within the group."

- **Have confidence in your ideas.** "First create your own value or innovative approach," advises Jyoti. Develop a track record. "If you are doing something useful and effective, then, sometimes, they [donors and supporters] will come to you," she says.

JENNIFER STAPLE

Mobilizing students worldwide to prevent blindness

UNITED STATES

I seek to empower youth throughout the world to reduce health inequities in their local communities. As a young person, I am passionate about improving the health and educational outcomes of young people everywhere. My goal is to motivate youth, both in the United States and internationally, to become leaders and create sustainable solutions to improve their communities.

– Jennifer Staple

As a college student, Jennifer Staple founded Unite for Sight to improve access to eye care services among disadvantaged people of all ages.

She fell in love with science in the seventh grade. That same year, a tragic television news story – about a boy dying after a car accident because he couldn't get enough air into his lungs – caught her attention. For her eighth-grade science fair project, she designed a machine for performing emergency tracheotomies. But it was not until she worked at an eye doctor's office in the summer after her first year of college that Jennifer Staple was transformed from merely a bright student with an interest in medicine into a passionate young activist with a mission.

The daughter of a computer businessman and a teacher, Jennifer grew up in a small town in the U.S. state of Connecticut, northeast of New York City. A gifted student, Jennifer already knew when she entered Yale University in 1999 that she wanted to pursue her interests in health and science, but she wasn't yet sure in which direction her studies would lead. Through that summer job with the eye doctor after her freshman year, she met dozens of low-income patients who came into the office for treatment. Conversing with these patients, Jennifer learned that many people with devastating eye diseases, including conditions that lead to blindness, could have prevented them with proper care and routine examinations. That simple realization changed her life.

Jennifer was transformed from merely a bright student with an interest in medicine into a passionate young activist.

Today, five years later, volunteers for Unite for Sight (UFS), the nonprofit organization Jennifer founded as a college sophomore in 2000, are providing eye care and educational programs around the globe. Currently active across the U.S. and in more than twenty-five countries, UFS has recruited more than four thousand volunteers worldwide. They are providing eye care for Sri Lankan victims of the tsunami that ravaged south Asia in December 2004; working in refugee camps to prescribe eyeglasses and deliver eye care to impoverished African, Asian, and Latin American communities; and screening for eye diseases in two Armenian towns. Jennifer herself recently organized the second annual Unite for Sight International Health Conference, an event at Harvard University that attracted more than four hundred health specialists, students, and public health and corporate leaders from across the United States and around the world.

Unite for Sight, which began in the United States, has expanded its operations to more than twenty-five countries.

Starting a Student-Led Project

Upon Jennifer's return to the Yale campus in New Haven after her summer job in the eye clinic, she founded Unite for Sight and recruited forty undergraduates as volunteers. That first year, she formed an executive board of students to help manage the fledgling organization. Their mission: to provide eye care to those who couldn't afford the services or who didn't have access to them.

Student volunteers visited soup kitchens and libraries to provide vision screenings. They engaged children by showing them diagrams of what the eye looks like and by letting them take apart a model of the eye and put it back together. "We tried to make the education programs fun, but also wanted them to learn how important it is to get eye exams by doctors," Jennifer recalls. Despite the necessity of working around their busy academic schedules, the students were able to reach more than two hundred people annually – carrying out community-based screenings.

Jennifer projects a deep sense of calm that was as remarkable when she was an undergraduate first launching UFS as it is now that she faces the pressures of managing a global organization. Dr. Shachar Tauber, an ophthalmologist with whom she worked at Yale, admits that he initially underestimated her determination. As Jennifer began to organize UFS, bringing world-class speakers to Yale University to speak about innovative research on eye diseases and eye health, he was impressed.

Building a Network

Unite for Sight is built around a fast-growing network of local chapters. In order to expand the program beyond New Haven, Jennifer emailed pre-medical curriculum advisors and student affairs offices at universities and colleges across the United States, informing them of her new organization and asking if they wanted to form chapters on their campuses. As a result, twenty-five new chapters were created during the summer of 2003, including ten in New York and six in Boston. Today, UFS has established more than ninety chapters at universities, medical schools, businesses, and high schools in the United States and around the world. Fittingly, its mission now includes empowering communities *worldwide* to improve eye health and eliminate preventable blindness.

In every location, the program, which is led and managed by students, relies completely on volunteers of all ages. Volunteers include elementary school students who collect used eyeglasses for distribution to those who can't afford them; high school students who educate their peers about proper eye health; and college and graduate students who conduct educational outreach and vision screenings in soup kitchens,

"We tried to make the education programs fun, but also wanted them to learn how important it is to get eye exams by doctors," Jennifer recalls.

There are now more than four thousand UFS volunteers worldwide, including nurses and doctors; public health officials; and high school, college, and graduate school students.

SECTION THREE
A Commitment to Grow: **From Local to Global**

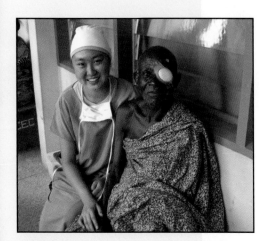

UFS is active in refugee camps in Ghana, where more than 150 patients have received sight-restoring cataract surgery.

homeless shelters, libraries, and community centers. Volunteers also include nurses, doctors, public health officials, and others with an interest in community and public health.

Each UFS program is tailored to meet the needs of its particular audience through programs and services that reduce health disparities and build the capacity of the local community. Chapters in North America and Europe implement vision screening and education programs and connect patients with free health coverage opportunities, so that they can receive complete eye exams by doctors. Internationally, local NGOs (nongovernmental organizations) and communities contact UFS after identifying acute eye care needs in their community and request a volunteer team to provide eye care and screening initiatives. Upon their arrival, UFS volunteers work directly with the local NGO to address the eye health needs of the community, while also organizing training sessions and seminars for children, adults, and teachers to ensure that local citizens become part of the global solution.

UFS chapters are self governing, electing their own officers and raising their own funds – from student government committees, college deans' offices, and community fundraising efforts. They are not,

however, autonomous. Volunteer members of each chapter adhere to a common set of rules and regulations, included in a "coordinator manual," and submit monthly updates on their activities to their regional director, who maintains close contact with every one of his or her chapters. The Unite for Sight organization itself raises funds for national and international efforts, through NGOs such as Global Youth in Action; international conferences attended by students, physicians, public health professionals, and corporate leaders; and individual donations. While UFS survived on less than U.S.$5,500 during 2003, by 2004 its budget had expanded to U.S.$150,000.

Each UFS program is tailored to meet the needs of its particular audience through programs and services that reduce health disparities in the local community.

Changing Lives, Restoring Hope

Unite for Sight's impact around the world has far exceeded Jennifer's dreams. The organization's volunteers have distributed more than thirty thousand eyeglasses and twenty thousand brochures on eye health worldwide. UFS has sponsored a growing number of eye operations as well.

"I see the trees and the gate to the eye center! I see the white gate, and I can tell you that it is open. Praise the Lord!" This was the excited cry of Lutee, a woman at the Buduburam Refugee Camp in Ghana, upon receiving sight-restoring cataract surgery. The operation was made available through UFS's cataract program, which has changed the lives of hundreds of villagers and refugees around the world.

"We work in very poor villages and refugee camps where no one can pay for eye care services," Jennifer explains, *"but we get so much in return."*

The international reach of UFS was initiated almost by chance. A medical school student, who had developed a relationship with a local NGO in Ghana, learned that in the village she was visiting, only one person owned a pair of eyeglasses – and even they were broken. To help address this urgent need, Jennifer decided to send a volunteer team to the village to provide eye care. And so began UFS's work in developing countries, where there is an enormous deficit in eye doctors and eye care.

In the West African nation of Benin, for example, there are only five eye doctors. Fewer than thirty such doctors operate in Tanzania. Yet many of

the eye diseases that ravage poor rural villages in the developing world, such as river blindness and trachoma, are preventable with simple antibiotics and treatable, if caught early enough, through surgery. All of the UFS health programs on five continents are designed to prevent blindness from cataracts, glaucoma, pterygium, vitamin A deficiency, and trachoma.

Activities in Ghana reflect the potential for impacting larger and larger numbers of people. In that one country alone, UFS has organized ten thousand eye screenings and distributed ten thousand pairs of sunglasses and eyeglasses. More than fifty blind patients in Humjibre, Ghana, and one hundred patients at Buduburam Refugee Camp have received sight-restoring cataract surgery. Reports one local resident: "There's a woman who lives in a cottage along the path that leads to my farm. She looked so frail that I thought ill health prevented her from going to the farm. I frequently said hello, but she was blind! Now her sight is restored."

Through their activities, UFS volunteers gain both inspiration and a profound learning experience. "We work in very poor villages and refugee camps where no one can pay for eye care services," Jennifer explains, "but we get so much in return." One man gave a UFS volunteer a live chicken as a sign of gratitude, Jennifer recalls. UFS volunteer Silvia Odorcic describes the response to the

UFS assesses the eye care needs within a community by conducting eye screening tests.

group's work in Ghana: "We were treated to more fruit than we could possibly consume, huge smiles, and gifts of gratitude." Sylvie Gardet, another volunteer, said that her experience restoring sight to blind patients "was the best thing I've ever done in my life."

UFS actively attracts volunteers through its website (www.uniteforsight.org) and local recruitment campaigns.

UFS places a priority on education programs that provide people of all ages with the knowledge and skills necessary to lead healthy lives. For example, to draw children's attention to certain foods they should eat to promote proper eye health, UFS volunteers now introduce the "pin the carrot on the eyeball" game (with "carrot" being replaced, as appropriate, by the local food that contains vitamin A). As always, a sense of fun is integral to the education process.

In addition to expanding its patient programs, Jennifer is turning UFS into an effective advocacy tool for improved eye health and disease prevention. She and her colleagues submitted a resolution to the American Medical Association in 2004 to encourage and support outreach efforts and to provide vision screenings for school-age children. Already adopted by the AMA's Medical Student Section, the resolution will be considered by the full AMA for adoption in 2005.

Looking to the Future

Jennifer, now 23, enjoys her current job as a full-time high school science teacher near her hometown in Connecticut. "I love motivating my students to develop creative ideas for science projects," she says, "and working through the scientific method to develop valid studies." She also continues to coordinate all of Unite for Sight's programs and volunteer activities. One can only wonder how Jennifer manages to contribute more than sixty hours a week to UFS from her office at home, in addition to her teaching obligations. She relies on email, instant messaging, and phone calls to help establish new chapters, develop partnerships, coordinate and manage programs, recruit volunteers, and promote outreach programs.

UFS volunteers make eye health education fun and engaging for young people by incorporating games and interactive exercises.

To ensure the sustainability and ongoing success of her organization, Jennifer deferred her enrollment at Stanford University School of Medicine, where she had been accepted in 2003. With her entrance into medical school in the fall of 2005, UFS is hiring its first full-time employee to coordinate all day-to-day activities. "I will continue leading the organization and managing the programs, but I will not have as much time for the daily tasks," Jennifer acknowledges. At Stanford, she will pursue a combined focus on public health and ophthalmology. Few who have met Jennifer doubt her capacity or commitment to reach her goals. Says Dr. Tauber, who now serves on UFS's medical advisory board, "Everyone she meets has been convinced by her commitment to improving people's lives; she simply captures their imaginations."

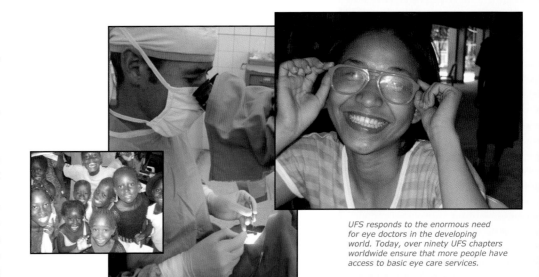

UFS responds to the enormous need for eye doctors in the developing world. Today, over ninety UFS chapters worldwide ensure that more people have access to basic eye care services.

What are Jennifer's long-term plans? "I would very much like to be a leader in the international health and ophthalmology fields," she asserts, "whether it's as surgeon general [the U.S. national spokesperson on public health issues], or a leader in the World Health Organization [WHO]." ∎

Over the centuries, most leaders have sought to bring about change through military intervention. I've tried to mobilize people to undertake another strategy – humanitarian intervention. Every citizen has the right to receive care and live with dignity, and national boundaries and political or financial circumstances cannot influence who receives that support. Through her work to expand the fight against blindness around the globe, Jennifer Staple has intervened in some of the world's poorest communities to ensure that their citizens, too, can lead healthy and productive lives.

Dr. Bernard Kouchner
Co-Founder Médecins Sans Frontières
Former Head UN Interim Administration Mission in Kosovo
Paris, France

ADVICE FROM JENNIFER ON:

Building and Expanding Your Organization

- **Take advantage of established networks to grow your organization.** UFS expanded its chapters by linking up with existing networks, including university organizations, medical deans' offices, international health networks, and nonprofit organizations. Jennifer says that UFS has strengthened its global reach by collaborating with such organizations as the International Federation of Medical Students' Associations and RESPECT International.

- **Educate and train your volunteers.** Says Jennifer, "Volunteers are the heart and soul of this organization, so we place a real priority on training and supporting them." All those interested in volunteering must first take the UFS online eye health course. Those who pass the final exam become UFS Eye Health Educators and are ready to educate their community about eye health and ways to prevent blindness. UFS also provides an online eye health curriculum, including games, on its website (www.uniteforsight.org) so that volunteers can more effectively work with children in school, and offers a training video to teach volunteers how to set up a vision screening program in their community.

- **Seek advice, and listen to it.** Critical components of the organization's ongoing success are its distinguished board of directors and medical advisory board. Says Jennifer, "I recruited an outstanding medical advisory board that has offered much-needed guidance over the years – about networking contacts and fundraising."

- **Leverage the power of the Internet to help in recruitment fundraising, and educating your constituency.** UFS's dynamic, user-friendly website offers clear directions for those who are interested in becoming active. UFS also widely disseminates an informative newsletter. Says Jennifer, "I spend much of my time emailing thousands of people on the Internet, contacting and recruiting new volunteers, and the website is a useful way for people to learn how they can become part of a global solution to improve eye health."

- **Create self-governing chapters who do their own fund-raising.** UFS currently has ninety self-sustaining chapters in the United States and around the world, and that number is growing

JAMES C. TOOLE, PH.D

PRESIDENT COMPASS INSTITUTE

James C. Toole, Ph.D. is President of the Compass Institute in Saint Paul, Minnesota, USA and a Teaching/Research Fellow in the University of Minnesota School of Social Work. This chapter is informed by a previous study of youth social entrepreneurs supported by the W.K. Kellogg Foundation.

Afterword
Reflections on How Youth Can Change the World

INTRODUCTION

Is there a collective meaning to the stories in this book? On the surface, the lives of these young people do not appear to be interconnected. They tell the stories of unique people in twenty countries addressing issues that are geographically and culturally diverse. One is trying to save a river in India, another to economically empower poverty-stricken men and women in Argentina, and yet another to teach music to children in Palestinian refugee camps. As Albania's Erion wisely warns, there are no franchise models in this work. The projects are "born" to specific people, places, and times.

Despite all this variation, six dimensions of leadership reoccur across the stories. They are the personal, visionary, knowledge, political, organizational, and societal. These dimensions provide not a recipe for youth-driven social change, but the naming of its main ingredients. The genius of these young people, as shown in the following discussion, is to mix and remix those ingredients to fit specific problems, people, places, and times in their particular country's history.

PERSONAL LEADERSHIP
Be the Change

The first dimension of leadership is personal character. Anyone who wants to change how a society thinks and acts will initially face skepticism or disinterest. Youth must at first sell not only an idea or a program, but themselves, to gain others' trust. Leadership therefore must involve both "inner" work (the person you are) and "outer" work (what you accomplish). When Albanian citizens stop Erion on the street to give him a hug and a thank-you, that personal connection serves a strategic purpose. Like Andrés and Agustín in Argentina, Erion finds that people support his organization both because of what he is doing and because of who he is. Why was Jennifer able to build Unite for Sight into a twenty-five-country network? Probably for two reasons: first, people sensed the gravity of the issue, and second, as one person shared about her, "she simply captures their imaginations."

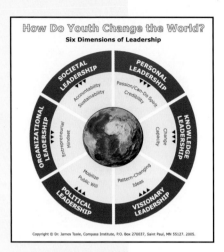

The young people described in this book demonstrate six dimensions of leadership, which they mix and remix to meet specific needs.

While youth leaders must therefore paradoxically both "sell themselves" and remain authentic, this is ultimately not a contradiction. These youth are naturally admirable. What emerges consistently is evidence of qualities such as passion, commitment, a can-do spirit, flexibility, creativity, high standards, playfulness, credibility, and integrity. The youth often ignore the magnets of financial security and professional prestige in favor of a societal mission. They combine a mentality that is at once quixotic and practical. They happily mix their home and work lives. They are courageous to confront attitudes covered by the dust of the past. They go to the library to study when there are no grades, no scholarships, and no credentials for their effort. They fight for issues that really matter (but not to other people). They are spiritual – in the sense that hope, compassion, and inclusion are spiritual. That they do all this and keep a sense of fun and play makes their purpose-driven lives enviable.

VISONARY LEADERSHIP
Be a Boundary-Breaker

The second dimension of this framework is visionary leadership. British playwright George Bernard Shaw's oft-quoted maxim is, "Some people see things as they are and say 'Why?' But I dream things that never were and say, 'Why not?'" Seinep dreamed of people with disabilities being given respect and opportunities in Kyrgyzstan. Stella dreamed of educating teens to prevent pregnancies and HIV/AIDS in Kenya. Jocelyn and Jessica dreamed of Canadians' changing their everyday lives in a hundred small ways to foster environmental sustainability.

Having a dream, however, is very different than becoming a change agent. Bill Drayton of Ashoka explains that the job of a change agent (what he calls a social entrepreneur) "is to recognize when a part of society is stuck and to provide new ways to get it unstuck." Youth are uniquely well adapted to play this role. They have what the Japanese call "beginner's mind." They see injustices, inconsistencies, and absurdities more quickly because they hold a different vantage point on society. For some of the youth in this book, that was because they lived the problem themselves. Other times they personally saw the impact on friends. Yet another group was moved by meeting people who were victims of that stuck society.

To get their societies "unstuck," the youth created pattern-changing ideas. Fittingly, Erion's organizational name translates as "Enough" and Maria's as "Interruption." Visionary leadership is about redirection. It is about both the process of change (think Dell's distribution system for its computers) and the end-goal (think Apple Computer's innovative products). As an example of "process" innovation, Jennifer set up a "distribution system" to deliver eye care in twenty-five countries. Marbie brought together three previously antagonistic Philippine tribes to work on sustainable agriculture. As an example of "product" innovation, Ha Thi Lan Anh started a youth-driven national radio show in Vietnam, where youth are traditionally taught that their place is to obey and respect their elders. Marbie's goal was to foster organic farming just at the time when the world was moving toward increasing use of chemical fertilizers.

KNOWLEDGE LEADERSHIP
Be a Learner

The third dimension of the framework is knowledge leadership. If you want to make a film like Harjant, you have to know not only film production, but also marketing and distribution. If you want to teach music to Palestinian children, it helps (like Ramzi) to have studied to become an internationally renowned musician. For MJAFT! to influence the Albanian government, Erion set up a policy branch to conduct research and make recommendations. Vimlendu started "completely clueless" about the pollution of India's Yamuna River, but spent weeks cloistered in the library to educate himself.

The message is clear. If you want to change the world, you have to study. The organizations in this book were, for the most part, founded by individuals who felt passionately about their cause (the poetry of change), but had little experience in management (the plumbing). They all realized that if you did your homework, as Ha Thi Lan Anh explained, "Then it will be harder for people to say no to you."

Once youth change agents acquired training themselves, they often created systems for volunteers, communities, funders, and the government to catch up. Julia used her teacher education to train volunteers on how to engage children with special needs. Jennifer set up an online health course for Unite for Sight volunteers. Ha Thi Lan Anh taught young reporters basic journalism skills.

Sometimes what is most interesting about a data set is what is missing. In all of these case studies, there is no mention that the youths' formal educations played a significant role in their projects. They spent hundreds of hours using the library, searching the Internet, conducting travel-study, and being mentored; but all on their own time. This raises the question about what schools might do to better foster and connect students' passion and work to the world around them.

POLITICAL LEADERSHIP
Be a Marketer and Collaborator

Innovative or transformative ideas are often born as orphans. Nobody initially recognizes them or claims them as their own. The goal of political leadership, the fourth dimension of the framework, is to mobilize public will – to turn orphan ideas into mainstream thought. That includes recruiting volunteers, forming cross-sector partnerships, securing media attention, and ultimately changing public opinion.

The projects in this volume span a wide range of issues. They include public health, the environment, youth development, economics, disabilities, agriculture, civic education, social marginalization, politics, and schooling. In all of these situations, members of the public were either unaware of the problem, didn't care about the problem, didn't think they could have an impact, or actively opposed any change. Addressing such perspectives is the job of political leadership.

How did these youth mobilize public will? They did so in multiple, inventive, and culturally specific ways. MJAFT! mobilized over one hundred people to cover the Albanian national telecom building

The goal of "political leadership" is to mobilize public will.

with toilet paper to protest poor management and high prices (prices were lowered). When a minister of the interior punched a journalist, MJAFT! sent instant messages on cell phones to over two hundred journalists, who ran to the Ministry to shake their keys and demand that the official be removed (he resigned).

The youth in these stories were engaged in social or cause-based marketing (i.e., the selling not of products, but of ideas, attitudes, and behaviors). As a young politician, Muhamed has faced widespread public pessimism in Bosnia and Herzegovina. He helped create an "I Love Tuzla" campaign and placed a bust of Martin Luther King Jr. in the town center. Jessica and Jocelyn's youth-oriented marketing included naming a program "Hopeful High School Hooligans" and constructing a website whose opening page pictures young people snoozing in sleeping bags. Kritaya spoke to Thai youth by writing a Top 40 "pop" song on changing the world.

Sadiqa faced some of the stiffest public opposition. How could she successfully advocate for female education in Afghanistan? She strategically invited mullahs and women to her home and based her case on the Qur'an. She quoted Mohammed's commandment to all people to be educated. On a personal note, she also told stories of female Afghan refugees in Pakistan and the United States who were unable to secure jobs, housing, or food because they couldn't read.

How we tell these stories about youth change agents can be misleading. What frequently gets overlooked is that even if an individual person does single-handedly invent a great idea, that innovation never becomes reality without the collective support, talent, and resources of many people. These stories, if one looks closely, are overflowing with supportive friends, mentors, foundations, and other community-based organizations. The nature of this work requires youth to be collaborators. As Harjant comments, "Just as it takes a village to raise a child, it takes a lot more than one person to make a successful feature or documentary."

ORGANIZATIONAL LEADERSHIP
Be an Entrepreneur

Ancient Chinese philosopher Lao Tzu realized long ago that weakness can sometimes produce power, and that power can foster weakness. The "weakness" of youth is that they may lack prior knowledge, resources, connections, and experience. What makes them organizationally powerful (the fifth leadership dimension) is that they are willing to see things in new ways, live on little money, turn their homes into offices, practice just-in-time learning, value the participation of other youth, seek partnerships, and enjoy new adventures. In most debates, this gives them the moral high ground – territory that is deeply im-portant when one is trying to change the world.

Otesha offers an excellent example of weakness as power. Sometimes not having funding can work to your advantage (many nongovernmental organizations, I'm sure, would beg to differ with me on this). Because the Otesha organization must rely on the kindness of people throughout Canada to support their cross-country bike rides – lending lawns to pitch tents and holding potluck meals to feed hungry riders – these hospitable strangers

Sadiqa employed various creative strategies in advocating for female education in Afghanistan.

become stronger supporters. If you want people to get involved and support your organization, you have to give them something meaningful (and in this case fun) to do. Otesha simultaneously secured free services and built their constituency.

These youth possessed many of the qualities identified with "social entrepreneurs" (those that use an entrepreneurial mindset to create social – rather than business – products and services). These qualities include being:

1. RESOURCEFUL. *No better example exists than Harjant, who made a moving, eight-minute film for less than U.S.$200. He recruited his twin brother as the lead actor, borrowed a friend's camera, and edited the piece on a computer in the public library.*

2. OPPORTUNISTIC. *Unite for Sight became an international organization "by chance." A medical school student learned through a local NGO in Ghana that nobody in an entire village had functional eyeglasses. To help address this essential need, Jennifer sent a volunteer team to provide eye care, and UFS's work in developing countries was born.*

3. "GEEKS." *There are multiple examples, already cited, of how these youth used cell phones, email, the Internet, and websites to help fulfill their mission. The message for change agents is clear: "Be a Geek." To see a compelling example, view Jennifer's website at www.uniteforsight.org.*

4. STRATEGIC. *When Ha Thi Lan Anh initiated a national radio program to educate her country about youth aspirations, she made a strategically sound move. Rural Vietnamese farmers listen to the radio over loudspeakers while they work in the fields, giving her a built-in audience.*

5. CULTURALLY FITTING. *In India, Jyoti campaigned to break cultural barriers for women to be leaders.*

She realized that she would gain more support if she was soft-spoken and assertive rather than loud and aggressive.

6. BIG PICTURE THINKERS. *The projects in this volume are at different stages of development, from small pilot efforts to large international organizations. In all cases, however, the youths' goal is not to form a successful organization, but to change their country in fundamental ways.*

7. PERSONALLY ORGANIZED. *Jennifer was able to teach school full time and spend sixty hours a week on Unite for Sight. Think about how organized she had to be!*

8. ACCOUNTABLE. *Social entrepreneurs continually focus on results. Several of the organizations built in systematic evaluations of the impact of their work.*

SOCIETAL LEADERSHIP
Be a Transformer

We live in a world where it is said that a butterfly that flaps its wings on one side of the planet ultimately affects the weather on the other side a month later. What this volume portrays is a different type of globalization – a globalization of youth-driven social and environmental change, or, as the International Youth Foundation calls it, a YouthActionNet. Its potential for convergence is too often overlooked.

These stories are important in their own right, but also for what they represent as a collective whole. It is provocative that youth in Albania and Argentina are simultaneously combating citizen apathy, that youth in India and the Philippines are struggling to clean up their environment, and that youth in Thailand and Mexico are involving young people in service learning.

The projects, while ranging from small pilot efforts to international organizations, each seek to change society in fundamental ways.

Perhaps what is most important to understand about their collective societal leadership is that, as European business writer Luc de Brabandere explains, "To change is to change twice." It is necessary both to change the world (reality) and how people see the world (perception). The first changes essential life conditions, but the second creates an environment in which much more can take place.

Tang understood this. He implemented a peer education program to prevent the spread of HIV/AIDS (i.e., the structure), but his deeper goal was to reduce the stigma and discrimination experienced by those with the disease in China (i.e., the culture). Likewise Seinep provided counseling and programs for disabled youth, but knew that her long-term goal was to secure public acceptance of rights for those with special needs. Ultimately, it is often small, grassroots social innovations like these that influence policymakers, governmental programs, and whole countries far beyond their humble beginnings.

Importantly, these youth not only changed their countries; they changed themselves. Jessica shared: "Looking at myself I can also see a very different person from the young woman who sat in despair almost three years ago. I hold the realization that there is nothing I would rather be doing, nothing that gives me more hope, than the work I am so privileged to do."

CLOSING

Michelangelo left a large number of his statues *non finito* (unfinished). The result is that these works seem to be in a constant state of emerging out of the marble. The statues offer a glimpse of the hope, beauty, and power that is possible through human imagination, while simultaneously conceding that the work is not yet over.

This is the same for the lives of those young people in this book, as well as for ourselves. Our work is still emerging out of the marble block that life has given each of us. Seinep's marble block was to be born with infantile cerebral palsy. Vimlendu's was to be born next to a great but polluted river. Tang Kun's was to be born shy, but to overcome that for a higher calling.

Their stories confirm not the "great people" theory of history, but that we are all called to lives of purpose and action. As Jocelyn shared: "We have learned that it is rare that youth are shown the power and opportunities they have today – everyday! – to work towards their ideal world, to truly be the change they want to see." These stories show what is possible if they are. Governments, schools, NGOs, international organizations, and foundations are left to explore how they can support many more youth globally to write their own stories of hope and societal progress. ∎

In China, Tang pursued a twofold approach: preventing the spread of HIV/AIDS and changing societal perceptions of those with the disease.

PHOTO AND ILLUSTRATION CREDITS

Through a dynamic website, an awards program, leadership training, and networking opportunities, YouthActionNet offers today's young leaders ideas, resources, and connections to like minds around the world.

The stories in this book are part of a larger unfolding story around the world of young people taking action to address urgent challenges in their communities. To learn about other youth engaged in positive change – or to order additional copies of this book – visit www.youthactionnet.org. Launched by the International Youth Foundation (IYF) and Nokia in 2001, YouthActionNet works to promote and strengthen the role of today's youth leaders and inspire others to make change.

Sponsoring Organizations

This book is a collaborative effort of the following organizations, which share a common commitment to promoting the role of today's young change-makers.

International Youth Foundation®

Founded in 1990, the International Youth Foundation is dedicated to supporting programs that improve the conditions and prospects for young people where they live, learn, work, and play. Currently operating in close to seventy countries and territories, IYF and its partners have helped millions of young people gain the skills, training, and opportunities critical to their success.
Visit: www.iyfnet.org

The philanthropic arm of Pearson plc, the Pearson Foundation extends the company's commitment to education, partnering with leading nonprofit, civic, and business organizations to provide financial, organizational, and publishing assistance to help teachers and young people across the globe. In addition to publishing this book, the Foundation is collaborating with IYF in the development of a companion online youth leadership curriculum to be made available through YouthActionNet.
Visit: www.pearsonfoundation.org

Through its cooperation with the International Youth Foundation and other regional philanthropic and social responsibility programs, Nokia prepares young people to embrace opportunities created by the global economy and new technological advancements. The company has been an active contributor to youth and education causes for many years and is the founding sponsor of YouthActionNet.
Visit: www.nokia.com

The *Laureate International Universities* network consists of eighteen campus-based and online institutions that provide career-oriented undergraduate and graduate programs to students in the Americas, Europe, and Asia. The Sylvan/Laureate Foundation is supporting the expansion of YouthActionNet's leadership development initiatives by launching the first YouthActionNet Institute in Mexico next year.
Visit: www.laureateuniversities.com